D0953148

DREAMING OUT LOUD

Baby Ariel
DREAMING OUT LOUD

HARPER

An Imprint of HarperCollinsPublishers

Library of Congress Control Number: 2018943093

ISBN 978-0-06-285748-4

Art direction by Alison Klapthor

Typography and design by Michelle Taormina

Interior illustations © 2018 by Ash & Chess

18 19 20 21 22   PC/LSCH   10 9 8 7 6 5 4 3 2 1

First Edition

For Jacob,
I love you from here to the stars and back again
(infinity times)

Table of Contents

Introduction

What's up, guys? It's Ariel! Welcome to my book!

I know most of you know me from social media, but it feels great to be here giving you a deeper glimpse into who I am behind the photos and videos. I've always been someone who loves to write stuff down and I've always been the most transparent in writing—there's something therapeutic about putting your thoughts on paper. I've been keeping journals since I was in preschool: every night at bedtime, I'd dictate to my parents and they'd write the words down for me. When I got to kindergarten and mastered the alphabet, it got a little easier. Now I probably have about twenty journals with my thoughts, ideas, and dreams for the future.

What I've always loved about keeping a diary is that I

could write about absolutely anything in the world, and the only person who got to read it was me. But that all changes with this book. *Dreaming Out Loud* is your chance to get to know me in a different way, to see what makes me excited and happy and even angry and sad. A little warning: I like to get creative and doodle in my journal—it just makes things so much more fun. So you'll also see my scribbles throughout the pages.

Right here up front I'll let you in on a little secret: the fact that I'm where I am today (thirty million followers on social media and three songs on the charts) is kinda crazy. What I want you to know is that I'm just a normal seventeen-year-old, and I have no idea how or why it all happened the way it did. But I do feel extremely blessed to be on this journey. Part of it is luck, I guess—being in the right place at the right time. The other part is being super comfortable with who I am and never being afraid to be uniquely myself. My parents instilled this mantra in me: dream big and dream out loud. Never hold back on what moves you, motivates you, makes you laugh, cry, or wanna scream. You gotta put yourself out there—which is one of the reasons I'm sharing all of this with you. I want you to become someone who isn't afraid to dream out loud. You have so much amazingness—why not share it with the universe? It's the key to social media success and the key to success in life in general: everyone has a voice, everyone has something to say, so *SAY IT!* (Get it? . . . SAY IT . . . YOU KNOW YOU LAUGHED.)

Another thing about *how* I dream: always in bright, vivid, splashy Technicolor. No black-and-white for me. You know when Dorothy arrives in Oz for the first time and everything is bursting with the colors of the rainbow? That's kinda how my mind works, even when I'm sleeping. So I organized this book into colored sections. If you're feeling blue, flip to the "I'm dreaming of . . . Blue" section for tips on how to cheer yourself up, boost your confidence, or survive an embarrassing moment. Do you have a huge crush on a guy or girl in school? The "I'm dreaming of . . . Red" section is where you go for romance and relationship advice.

I want you to take your time going through these pages and, if something speaks to you, let it inspire your own story. That's the thing: we all have stories to tell, which is why I love Story Time videos so much and make a whole lot of them for you on my YouTube channel! These are videos about moments in my life that I can't forget (even if I really, really want to). This entire book is about those moments. Some are pretty random, while others are about people and places and things that stand out in my mind as an experience that shaped the person I am and the person

I'm becoming. I wanted to fill every chapter with what makes me tick, and all my observations and opinions about the ups and downs and the struggles I have been through along this journey. At least, the journey so far—there's a long, winding road still ahead! I'm excited to see where it takes me, and I hope you are, too.

xo,

Ariel x

(P.S. I highly recommend reading this book while eating white cheddar popcorn, it's the best snack in the world, just saying.)

I'm dreaming of WHITE

WHITE is the color of new beginnings, fresh starts, infinite possibilities—a blank page to write and sketch.

oh, baby!

So this is how it all started

I was born on November 22, 2000, at 2:22 p.m. at Memorial Hospital West in Pembroke Pines, Florida. I still live in the same area today in a four-bedroom, one-story house with a pool in the backyard, along with my mom, my dad, my brother, Jacob, and my puppy, Bleu (a crazy, fluffy white Maltipoo). My dad, Jose, is from Panama, and my mom, Sharon (pronounced Sha-rone), was born in New Jersey. My mom's parents are from Cuba and Israel, while my dad's were born in Spain and Panama. I've also got Russian, Czechoslovakian, and German blood running through me.

My mom described me as "the sweetest soul," when I was a baby, always perfectly happy and content. My name means "lioness of God," which I think is pretty fierce, and my parents nicknamed me Wiggle Worm and Gushy Monster. I loved to snuggle up with my stuffed bunny, and my favorite toy was a marching Mickey Mouse doll that sang a parade song when you squeezed his hand. I had the biggest blue eyes and the chubbiest cheeks. My parents called me their Curious George, always wide-eyed and crawling around everywhere—especially places I wasn't supposed to be, like under tables or inside the kitchen cabinets. When I still had zero teeth, I loved applesauce and mashed banana. But judging from some of my high chair pics, I wore more of my meal than I ate. I would also finger-paint the tray of my high chair with all my colorful cuisine—such an *artist*.

Mom tells me I had the biggest sense of humor for a little kid. Whether something was funny or not, I always laughed and tried my hardest to make people crack up. Case in point: as a toddler, I decided for a while that I was Tarzan. Did I care that Tarzan was a *guy* who lived in a jungle with apes and sported long hair and a loincloth? I think . . . NOT. I loved the Disney movie so much, I would literally undress myself and run around in public in my underwear, banging on my chest and doing the Tarzan call as I jumped from the couch to the chair, swinging my jump rope like a vine. Now I like to tell silly jokes to people all the time and try to make them laugh. Here, I'll tell you my favorite:

"Knock, knock!"

"Who's there?"

"Britney Spears."

"Knock, knock!"

"Who's there?"

"OOPS, I DID IT AGAIN!!"

Very stupid, but VERY FUNNY, I know.

My little brother, Jacob, was born when I was three. I was super excited to be a big sister and I somehow managed to appear in the delivery room while he was being born. No one noticed me standing there because they were all facing my mom, who was, you know, a little preoccupied herself. Eventually, in the middle of the delivery, Mom looked up and saw me standing there, wide-eyed, and said, "Hi, angel!" But then some nurse grabbed me and shuffled me out the door, and I missed Jacob's big entrance. Still, I loved that kid from the time he was in my mom's tummy. I know a lot of siblings who fight constantly, but I consider myself lucky to get along so well with my brother. When we do argue, it's usually over something stupid, like him barging into my room without knocking or hogging the AUX in the car for his music. Jacob and I have many similarities, which is why we get along. Our differences also bring us closer because we lean on each other for advice. For example, I am very stubborn and sometimes I need Jacob to remind me to be more open and forgiving. Likewise, I am there to encourage him to share his feelings when he closes up and wants to sit in his room and sulk. Our similarities tend to be on the creative side. We both love to read, write, watch movies, and go to the theater. We feel strongly about the need to express ourselves. He's fourteen, and I know from experience that life can get complicated right about now. I'll always be there for him.

My parents have always encouraged us to "do what you love and love what you do." That's probably one of the best pieces of advice anyone has ever given me, because it's allowed me the freedom to change direction and try new things fearlessly. When I was younger, I was all about dance and playing the piano. Then, when I got older and decided to give up both to try a sport, my parents didn't flinch; they just signed me up for soccer and got me some cleats (even after all the money and time they poured into my music and dance lessons!). They've always allowed me to make those choices, to follow my heart and my dreams wherever they led me, and to figure out what truly brings me joy. I consider myself blessed to have such open and nurturing parents. Jacob and I can always go to them about absolutely anything and there's no judgment. They want us to be true to ourselves and live the lives *we* envision—not what they envision for us. That support has made me feel free to explore, to experiment, to be crazy, to figure out what I want to be and do it—with no limitations or hesitations.

I've always had very strong opinions about almost everything, and in our house, we are free to speak them. We have long talks about religion, psychology, politics, you name it, usually over the dinner table and my mom's famous mussels and scallops. You never have to twist my arm to spend time with my family—I really enjoy our time together. We love watching *Big Brother* and *The Goldbergs* and playing Yahtzee and Clue on family game night. The only time I *do* fight with my mom and dad is when they pry about something I'm going through before I'm ready to share it with them. I'm someone who tries to handle everything by myself; I've always been like that. So when I am working through a problem about a friendship, my career, or a boy I have a crush on—I don't like to open up about my issues until I've worked them out.

Because my parents have always been good about letting

me have my say and do things my way, I'm an outside-the-box kind of person. It's one of the reasons I'm homeschooled. In my experience, some traditional schools force you to play by a concrete set of rules and regulations. There's a rigidness to how things are done, and as organized and disciplined as I am, I like a little wiggle room. Sometimes I felt bored and unchallenged in class; my mind tended, even when I was little, to race at a hundred miles per hour. I was a good kid and a good student and I never got in trouble because I was also really good at not getting caught when I misbehaved! My favorite subjects were English and history, mainly because both involved storytelling. I didn't have to pretend to listen in those classes because I was always engaged. I absolutely loved writing personal narratives—"What I did on my summer break" was a favorite because I could tell all the fun, crazy details of my adventures. In ninth grade, my history teacher, Mrs. Ibanez, would tell us tales of queens and kings and epic battles as if she was reading from a fairy tale not a textbook. She literally brought history to life for me; I could picture it playing out like a movie. For obvious reasons, I loved show-and-tell and oral presentations—it gave me the opportunity to stand up and talk in front of a captive audience. My playdates were also performance opportunities: my best friends in elementary school were Ashley and Sophie, and they both loved dance as much as

I did, so we staged intricate recitals, complete with original choreography and costuming, and made our poor parents watch and applaud enthusiastically.

It's funny, but when I look back on my childhood, I see so many hints of the person I am today. There may not have been a musical.ly when I was little, but I was still performing, hamming it up for an audience, spinning stories, and pushing the envelope. I am content with who I am but still consistently striving to better myself and to grow and learn. I will always stay true to myself; I will not compromise or morph into something I'm not in the name of fitting in.

Story Time

A TRIP DOWN MEMORY LANE (OUCH!)

One of my earliest memories is from when I was seven years old. We were on our annual family camping trip to beautiful Collier-Seminole State Park with one of our closest family friends, the Marcuses. Some of my fondest memories from these outings were barbecuing, splashing around the lake, and building a fire every night and roasting s'mores over it. While the very idea of camping would have scared many of my friends, I looked forward to our trip every year. I loved sleeping in a tent, going hiking, canoeing, and telling stories by the campfire. I never minded bugs or dirt or worried about some wild animal attacking us in the middle of the night.

On this particular trip, for some reason my dad decided to take on the task of teaching me to ride a bike—a pink two-wheeler that was a hand-me-down from my cousin Alexandra. I wasn't all that psyched to ride a big-girl bike, but I idolized Alexandra and wanted to be her when I grew up. She's only three years older than me, but back then it felt like an enormous age difference, and she had a maturity about her that mesmerized me. She was in middle school; I was still languishing in third grade. She was an accomplished dancer; I was not. We went to all her recitals, and I looked up to her like a big sister.

For these reasons, the fact that the bike had been Alexandra's made it magical. Dad packed it in the trunk of the car for the trip, and when we got there, he pulled it out and asked me to follow him to the top of a hill on the campground. I knew what was going to happen next: he was going to give me a shove off that hill and let go. *Bye, Ariel!*

"Nothing can go wrong as long as you keep pedaling," he told me. And I believed him! I pedaled and pedaled, looking over my shoulder to make sure he was still hanging on to the back of the seat, running along beside me.

"I think you've got the hang of it!" Dad called to me. "I'm gonna let go now and you can take it from here!"

Bad idea. Really bad idea. Worst idea ever. Thanks, Dad.

Once he released his grip, I lost control of the bike (. . . duh). I swerved left, then right, sped out of control, panicked, and screamed my seven-year-old head off because I couldn't keep my balance or work the brakes, and eventually the bike flipped over. I landed at the bottom of the hill, face-first.

My dad, to his credit, chased after me and tried to grab hold of the back of the bike when he saw things were clearly not going as planned. But he missed and tumbled over as well. When I stood up, blood was gushing out of my mouth, and a huge chunk of my gum was ripped above my tooth. It was badass, if very painful.

When we went back the next day (glutton for pain and punishment that I am!), I was even more determined. I was going to keep that bike steady and not freak out. I was going to be calm and cool and glide down that hill like a pro—even if it killed me (literally). So we started the exact same way: Dad pushing and me pedaling, and both of us dreading the inevitable moment when he would turn me loose. But when he did this time, I didn't panic. I wobbled and tried to steady the handlebars, but I kept on pedaling, eventually finding just the right position on the seat with my butt cheeks firmly planted. And that was it—I was riding. All by myself, two wheels, hair blowing in the wind. It felt *ah-may-zing*! I did it again and again, each time steadier and more confident than the time before.

This whole bike drama taught me a really important lesson: I can't ever, EVER let fear hold me back. I may get a few battle scars for my efforts, but that's okay. Finding your balance in life—on a bike or otherwise—is so worth it.

In every chapter, you'll find these boxes filled with my tips, tricks, and advice for tackling all the tough stuff in life. Take it one step at a time. . . .

Baby Steps

STICK TO YOUR GOALS LIKE KRAZY GLUE!

Some people are born experts: they can master the violin the first time they pick it up or spell "onomatopoeia" without ever googling it. But for the rest of us ordinary people, most things don't come that easy. We have to practice . . . and practice . . . and practice some more. I had to practice singing every day just to get comfortable enough with my voice to step into a studio and record. I'm still not where I want to be, but I'm slowly and surely getting there. And I know the more I work at it, the better I'll become. And I don't plan on ever stopping. Most times the reason we have to do things over and over is simply because it's new, uncharted territory. You won't get it—not at first, and maybe not even after the tenth or eleventh try. But that's no reason to quit. You've gotta believe quitting is never an option. When I put my mind to something, I go for it with every ounce of energy and all my determination and passion.

If you can see it, you can be it. I'm a big believer in visualizing what I want to achieve. It's like creating an Instagram feed in your brain: you see images of yourself living your dream, following your passion, doing what you love the most. Anytime I feel doubt or insecurity sneaking up on me, I just go to this imaginary happy place where I can *see* myself succeeding. If you put those thoughts out in the universe, the universe can't help but pitch in and give you a hand.

Give yourself a pep talk. When you wake up in the morning, don't lie there in bed, beating yourself up or whining. Be your own cheerleader. There are days I'm nervous, days I'm doing an important interview or speaking at an event, and I'll tell myself, "Okay, Ariel. Do not freak out. You got this." Thoughts have energy, so make yours count. And just know that confidence is contagious. The minute you put out there that you got this, other people will believe it, too.

No pressure. Because I've always been so determined, my mom cautions me not to be hard on myself and reminds me that achieving goals takes time. Dream as big as you like, but see it through little by little. Tell yourself that each thing you do, no matter how small or insignificant it feels in the moment, is getting you closer and closer to the finish line. Like I said, I've been eager to get my singing career going, but you can't just release a record overnight. It takes time to find the right people to work with, figure out the right songs, and get it to sound the way I want it to. I feel like I've had a lot of stops and starts because I want the music I put out to be the best it can be, and sometimes, yeah, I get impatient. But you have to be realistic and allow yourself plenty of time to experience some setbacks along the way. Which brings me to . . .

Failure doesn't define who you are. Mistakes are part of the learning curve; it's totally normal to mess up a few (gazillion) times before you figure things out. If I'd said "nah" after that first bike crash, I would never be able to bike around my neighborhood with friends—which is one of my favorite things to do. It's okay to feel anxious, frustrated, even fed up. Just don't let those emotions control you; *you* show them who's boss.

#askAriel

You know you can ask me anything and I'll give you my completely, 1,000 percent, honest opinion, right? In every chapter, I have chosen a few of your weirdly random yet wonderful, super-challenging questions to respond to.

When you grow up, get married, and have a kid, will you change your name to "Mama Ariel"? And will your kid then be "Baby Ariel?"

Hmmm, that's a really good question and definitely one I've never thought about before. I guess I gotta grow up sometime and pass down the title—kind of like the queen of England handing over the throne one day? There is one thing I do know: if I have a girl, I'm naming her Leila (it means "night" in Hebrew). Any guy who marries me better be okay with that because there are no ifs, ands, or buts about that one.

If you could be any Disney princess, who would you be and why?

This will shock you, I know, but I'd have to say Ariel, the Little Mermaid. Or maybe Princess Jasmine from *Aladdin*. I love that they're both independent, adventurous girls who want to see the world and aren't afraid to venture out of their comfort zones. And both can seriously sing!

Why do you hate cheese? It's so good!

Accounts of my alleged cheese hating is something I'd like to clear up once and for all. I do not hate cheese—I just don't like it *melted*. I love shredded Parmesan that comes in those little zip and reseal bags at the supermarket, and sliced cheddar that you buy at a deli counter. Oh, and the powdered cheese that comes with Easy Mac that you add hot water to and mix up with the noodles? Love it. But melted cheese, the stuff they glop on top of pizza? HECK NO. Same goes for lasagna, baked ziti, chicken Parmesan . . . if it includes melted cheese, it's just not for me.

The app that changed my life

It was May 2015, just when school was ending and summer was starting. A pipe burst under our kitchen sink and our house flooded, so we had to move out. Needless to say, I was not very happy. We had to move in temporarily with my mom's parents, Safta (Hebrew for "grandma") and Papa, who live just a few blocks from us.

There I was, living out of a suitcase in a little room in my grandparents' place, feeling bored and restless. To pass the time, I went on my phone and looked through pictures and videos on Instagram. While scrolling one day, I saw a lip-synch video a friend of mine made on an app called musical.ly. It immediately intrigued me and I wanted to give it a try, so I downloaded the app and started to play around. People always ask how I came up with my muser name. I really wish I had some exciting story to tell you because it's a question I get so often. But honestly, it was all very random. I saw some other girls on the app calling themselves "Queen So and So," and "Lil This or That" and figured I should have a cute nickname. Inspired by my cousin Katia, whose email address started with the words "BabyKatia," I went ahead and picked "Baby Ariel" and figured, "Well, I'll just change it later." But it kind of stuck and that's how people came to know me.

I thought it was such an interesting app and I'd never seen anything like it. I'd seen how on Instagram people posted great pictures, and on Vine (RIP) people made funny six-second clips. But I'd never seen an app where you could make longer videos (fifteen seconds back then) and put them to music. I started watching a lot of those early musical.ly videos and the amount of creativity and fun was inspiring to me. But I also felt like I could do things differently than what I was seeing. I saw most people just kind of singing along to the music trying to look cute or pretty. They felt like "lip-synch selfies." I thought, "What if I give each video more meaning? What if I make it more interesting to watch? How could I do that?"

So I started to think creatively. With musical.ly there's a way where you can slow the video down while you record but play it back at regular speed. It's an awesome visual effect. I thought it'd be cool to record that way while including precise hand movements to go along with the words. And to top it off, I'd get really expressive with my face.

I wanted it to be almost like a musical sign-language ballet. When I was young, my parents, who both studied film and acting, showed me old silent movies with Charlie Chaplin. They would point out how much could be said with just facial expressions and body movement. I thought I could do something like that with this cool new app. That first day when I was just starting out, I found one of my favorite songs by Nicki Minaj and posted my first video and continued to post daily over the next couple of weeks. I planned out each video's hand movements and facial expressions, and was very particular about how I moved my phone camera. Believe it or not, some of those fifteen-second clips took over an hour to plan and execute! After those few weeks on the app, one of my videos got featured. My video was spotlighted on the home page and my exposure jumped from my roughly eighty followers of family and friends to thousands of users. I was beyond excited! My family, my biggest (and only) fans at the time, was as elated as I was, if not more so! But I had no way of knowing what a huge impact being featured would have on my life; at the time I was just thrilled to be recognized for my efforts. Over the next few weeks, my profile grew to over twenty-five thousand followers and continued to get featured. By the end of the summer, I had over one and a half million followers.

I could hardly wrap my brain around that astronomical number; that's an insane amount of people who were watching me.

I started doing my YouTube videos because I wanted my followers to get to know the real me—fifteen-second clips of me lip-synching expresses my creativity, but not who I am as a person. My followers knew the music I loved, but not much more. I started researching a lot of other social media people. I watched Miranda Sings and Tana Mongeau, and other successful YouTubers and I realized, "Okay, they don't *only* do YouTube. They don't *only* do Instagram, or Twitter, or muscial.ly." I figured out that you need different outlets to express different sides of yourself. So I sat down and filmed a YouTube video, just like that. It was a Q & A and I was pretty awkward and clearly didn't have a clue what I was doing. I had people send me questions about absolutely anything they wanted to know, everything from "What kind of car does your mom drive?"

to "Have you ever kissed a boy?" It didn't mean I had to stop doing musical.ly; it just meant adding another layer to what I already did. It was another way of expressing myself, another form of creativity. I find that each medium showcases a different side of me—and that's the beauty of it. If you want to build a social media following, you have to be willing to be 100 percent genuine.

I won't kid you: it can be scary. You open yourself up to people who may not get you or understand what you're doing or why you're doing it. When I do my videos, I'm sharing some pretty revealing, intimate stuff. Some people might ask, "Why? Why would you want to divulge your innermost thoughts to a ginormous group of random strangers?" Well, I love it—simple as that. There is an incredible feeling of freedom that comes from being your authentic self and sharing that with others. A lot of my inspiration comes from my life and the crazy things that always seem to happen to me. Seriously, it's like I'm living an *I Love Lucy* episode. I can laugh at all my bloopers and blunders, and I always want to make people happy and put a smile on their faces. I know it's something I'm meant to do and I don't regret anything I've ever said or posted (except maybe the video where I talk about peeing my pants). But beyond that, I am really, truly okay with everything I put out there. My family has gotten used to it as well; we have all become accustomed to sharing our experiences no matter how silly or embarrassing.

The most important thing is to do *you* and not worry about what people might think. Put yourself out there because you want to do it, not because you're seeking approval, friends, followers, or comments. Do it because it brings you joy . . . period. Don't obsess over the number of people liking or following you—that's kind of secondary. If you are your true self, I promise they will come. In my case, I never dreamed so many people would be following me. All I kept thinking was, "What? Really? Wait . . . how? Why?"

I honestly don't know the answers to those questions. I've watched my early musical.lys and I just see me, having fun, doing it my way, which is all I've ever done and know how to do. Maybe it was a little different from what other people were doing on the app, and that's what sparked the interest: "Who is this girl? What's up with that? That's kind of cool . . ." It was the very beginning of Baby Ariel, the moment in time I can point to and say, "Oh, yeah, that was when everything changed for me." In a lot of ways it was a personal validation: *Hey, Ariel, what you love to do, what makes you happy: it makes other people happy, too!* Publicly becoming Baby Ariel set the wheels in motion for my entire career: doing musical.ly led to my first DigiFest tour, and that led to me creating my YouTube channel, where I could actually use my voice (not lip-synch to someone else's) and share who I am with the world. It's all happened at hyperspeed. I still make musical.lys every day, but they're not all I do anymore. I like to think that they're a piece of me, but there's more to the bigger picture. I am always working to improve myself. I read a lot, I take performance and acting classes, and I'm working on my singing career and writing daily. Basically, I'm someone who is never content with mastering one thing. As soon as I do, I am ready for the next challenge; I'm all about "so, now what?" Will everything work out for me to the extent that musical.ly or my videos have? Maybe not. But that doesn't mean I stop learning and growing. I am extremely grateful that I started on musical.ly at the beginning of the app's popularity and that I struck a chord with my unique style. I didn't realize it at the time of course, but in retrospect I was appreciated for being my true self, because I was doing it for myself. To be "different" means some people are gonna love you and some aren't, and you have to be able to handle both outcomes. In my case, I wasn't purposely trying to be different; I was just inspired and I went for it. As I've come to know my audience, I feel like we've come to understand each other. I hope I'm there to help lift them up and bring them joy when they're down, and they do the same for me when I need a boost. They want me to be myself and share my personal experiences because (guess what?) they're just like everyone else's. I'm a real person; I screw up a whole lot and freak out and I'm not afraid to admit it. Case in point: the infamous tampon incident.

This has become one of my classic Story Time videos, and I know many of my followers have watched it repeatedly because it cracks them up. In the moment when it was happening to me, I was not very amused, but after making a YouTube video about it, now I can laugh along with everyone else.

So, I was sixteen years old, the *only* girl on tour, and hanging out with some of my best friends, who happen to be a bunch of boys: Weston, Nathan, Blake, and Mark. Now ask yourself: What's the worst thing that could happen when you're surrounded by a bunch of cute boys, trying to act cool? You guessed it: I got my freakin' period.

I panicked and announced, "Guys, I need you to go downstairs and get me some pads—this is an emergency!" Even mention you're menstruating and boys squirm. They know girls have periods; they just don't want to know the details. There I was, shoving them out the door, forcing them on a quest for feminine hygiene products, stat. They returned triumphantly from the hotel lobby shop with Tampax. For the record, I didn't ask for tampons but that was all the store had.

"Thanks," I said, staring at the small box. I had never used a tampon before, but it was my only option. So into the bathroom I went, phone in hand, to do some research. Now let me preface this by saying *before* all of this went down, I had had my phone connected to the Bluetooth speaker in the hotel room and had been playing music.

I sat down on the toilet and googled "how to put in a tampon." For the record, there are dozens of videos out there on the subject because, at some point, a girl just needs to know. I found one that was pretty simple to follow and watched it intently. I got the tampon in, and I thought I was good to go. But then I came back into the room and all the guys were staring at me.

"What?" I asked, confused. "What did I miss? What happened?"

They all smirked. "Check Twitter."

I went on Twitter, and sure enough, I saw a tweet from Weston that was getting tons of engagement. As I started watching his tweet, I instantly realized what had happened: because I'd been connected to the Bluetooth speaker earlier in the day, the step-by-step instructions I was listening to in the bathroom had played on the speaker for the boys to hear, too! And Weston had recorded it all and tweeted it out to the world. Now, it's embarrassing enough to have a bunch of boys listening to your tampon instruction story. But now the whole world knew? For the record, Weston is one of my all-time closest friends. He's like a little brother to me and I love him to death. But don't worry, I'll get him back! To say I was humiliated would be putting it mildly. But now that it was already out there on Twitter, there was only one logical thing I could do. I had to make my own YouTube video about the experience because when life hands you lemons (and you're me), ya gotta post it!

Story Time

THE UBER RIDE FROM HELL

Okay, maybe not everyone broadcasts tampon tutorials over Bluetooth, but there have been many other moments when I've posted a video that people can easily relate to. I made a video about getting a bad haircut, about my first kiss in seventh grade, about learning to drive. Since the start, it has been a priority to show my supporters that we ALL go through crazy, scary, and sometimes unfortunate events, but in the end, we will survive. Nothing is off-limits—and I mean nothing. In fact, the more harrowing the experience, the better the video. You can't make this stuff up. Like the very first time I took an Uber by myself. Most people just get in, buckle up, get out. Not me. It was a horror story. So, put on your seat belt and get ready for this wild ride of a story . . . GET IT? . . . YOU LAUGHED.

In this day and age, taking a car service solo is a teenage rite of passage, especially if, like me, you live in or are visiting a big city. Basically, if you're not licensed to drive yet in LA, you either have to get a ride from your mom, ask a friend, or get an Uber. So I knew the day would come—and to be honest, I wasn't looking forward to it. Being alone with a strange driver in an enclosed space made me nervous. My mom was also making me paranoid doing the overprotective "I'm your mother and it's my job to worry" thing. She gave me a laundry list of instructions: "Send me a screenshot of the driver's ID! Make sure you check and double-check the license plate number and ask who he is picking up. Don't get in if he looks creepy. . . ."

So when the Prius pulled up and I climbed in, I had to give the driver a quick once-over to gauge his Creep Quotient. My exceptional mentalist/profiling skills told me the guy was about thirty and I made sure to commit his face to memory—just in case I had to identify him in a future FBI lineup. I should probably come clean here and admit I have watched way too many episodes of *Criminal Minds*, which is why I assume any stranger has sketchy, psychopathic potential. But Mr. Uber didn't seem that way: he was friendly and courteous and even started chatting me up:

"So, how you doing?"

"Good."

"You having a nice day so far?"

"Yup."

"You from around here?"

Up until this moment, I had tried to be polite and respond with single-word answers without getting into my whole life story. Naturally, he wanted to get into my whole life story.

"When did you move here? Who do you live with? How old are you—I bet you're nineteen."

"No, I'm sixteen," I stupidly volunteered. I could hear my mom's voice ringing in my ears: "Don't talk to strangers!"

"What? You're only sixteen? You're so beautiful!"

So at this point I was thinking, "This guy is a homicidal maniac/serial killer who is about to kidnap me and I will never be seen or heard from again." This wasn't just a quick ride down the block, so I had plenty of time to run through all the worst-case scenarios in my head. I was traveling about thirty minutes to my destination, and the trip took us up and down the Hills. This guy was riding the curves like a roller coaster—he would speed up, slow down, lurch to a sudden stop. I made sure my seat belt was fastened tightly, held on to the door for dear life, and started to prepare for my impending death.

"So, you been here long?" he continued prying. "What brings you to LA?"

If the game of Twenty Questions wasn't bad enough, then all of a sudden he started taking a different route (I knew this because I was staring at my Uber app the whole trip). That's when I started to *really* panic. I texted my mom, "Oh my god, he's going the wrong direction! What do I do?" While I waited for her to text her reply (she types painfully slow), I decided I needed to speak up and do something.

"Hey, where are you going?" I asked. I tried to open the windows (in case I had to scream for help) but they were locked. "Could you please open the window," I requested sweetly, trying to downplay the fact that I was having a major panic attack in the back seat. He assured me everything was fine, but I was so *not* fine and now my mom was calling me every twenty seconds, freaking out as well. Finally, his GPS said we were five minutes away from my destination, and I breathed a huge sigh of relief.

"You mind if I stop and use the bathroom?" he suddenly asked me.

Wait, what? Are you kidding me? We're almost there and you want to pull over to some strange, random gas station and pee? You want to prolong this horror story for ten more minutes?

"Uh, no. Drop me off first," I insisted. "I'm late."

When he dropped me off, I swear, all I wanted to do was kiss the ground because I was so thankful I had survived! I took several deep, cleansing breaths, then related the whole

    ✦

ordeal to my friends and to my mom, who I had called to report my safe arrival. Since that day, I've had a few other creepy cab rides—probably even worse than this one—but I'm more experienced. I don't panic; I just remain on high alert. Did I overreact? Probably, but I'm glad to have shared my horrifying experience with everyone as a precautionary tale.

I just hope my Uber driver didn't watch it.

Baby Steps

THE KEY TO MAKING
A MASTERFUL MUSICAL.LY

What I love about musical.ly is that it encourages creativity and imagination, whether you choose to lip-synch to a song, do a comedic skit, or create your own original content; no matter how you use it, it should always be infused with your own personal style. It's a chance for you to perform and shine and be original.

Because I became known on musical.ly for doing lip-sync videos, I've done quite a few tutorials on the subject on YouTube. Here are some of my best tips:

- **Whether you choose a song you know or challenge yourself with a new one, learn the lyrics.** You need to know the lyrics by heart so you can give your best performance. If you don't have it memorized, listen to it over and over until you get it down.

- **Play the song through and plan out what hand motions and facial expressions you want to use.** The song has all the clues you'll need: What actions are being spoken? For example, if someone sings, "Hit me up!" you might want to position your hand like you're talking on a phone. For your face, you want to channel the emotions the artist is thinking or feeling. Is he or she sad, angry, excited, etc.? Analyze the lyrics and focus on the parts that inspire you. The lyrics of most songs tell a story and doing a musical.ly is your opportunity to share your favorite parts!

- **Location, location, location.** Your bedroom might not be the best place to shoot—although I certainly have made many videos in front of my purple walls. It's fun to find a unique place (The grocery store? Your school gym? Back seat of a car when mom is driving?) to make your video stand out. I love making musical.lys in the car with my dog, Bleu. The other really fun thing to do is "jump cut" to different locations within a musical.ly. Start the musical.ly in one spot, then transition within the song to another location. Do that multiple times within a musical.ly and it is a great effect!

- **Break the song into "chunks"—don't try and record it all at once.** The video will be way too long and you'll feel overwhelmed. A verse or two and a chorus is plenty.

- **Don't just stand there.** Move the phone in the same direction you are pointing/directing. Make circles with it; shake it up. This creates cool camera angles and movement.

- **Express yourself.** Exaggerated facial expressions look great on musical.ly. Try not to be self-conscious. I roll my eyes, purse my lips, wrinkle my nose, stick out my tongue: whatever I'm feeling, I use my face to show it— no matter how goofy I look (and trust me, I look pretty goofy).

- **Listen for the beat changes; you can use them to kick off transitions.** One trick I like is to go from regular playback speed to slo-mo. Shake the camera, switch the speed from fast to slow—then shake it again.

- **Use props.** One of the most popular videos I did was to the song "Popular" from the musical Wicked. I think it resonated with fans because I used props like makeup and shoes and really acted it out. I channeled my inner Glinda!

- **You can always delete it later.** I cringe at some of my old musical.lys! Just know that you can always go back and get rid of older ones once you sharpen your recording and editing skills.

- **Experiment and take risks.** If you want to improve your skills, practice each day and try new things, collaborate with friends, and play with camera angles. The beauty of musical.ly is you can record over and over and watch it back without posting if you aren't happy with how it turns out.

- **And most importantly!! Be yourself!** Authenticity is what people gravitate toward, whether online or in real life. So, just be you and have fun.

#askAriel

I want more followers on my YouTube vlog—how do I get them?

Before you worry about gaining followers on YouTube or any platform, make sure you're doing it all for the right reasons: you enjoy making content and you want to express yourself. People will sense whether you're making content that is "true to you" or "just to get big" and will be put off if it's for the wrong reasons. So once you feel you are doing it for the right reasons, I can give you this advice. Somebody once explained it to me like this: think about your favorite TV show and how you look forward to the day/time it's on every week. That is how you should think of your posts. Your followers want to know when you're posting so they can anticipate the content and tune in—they want consistency and you need to give it to them. You can also brand your vlogs so followers know what to expect on certain days: maybe Sunday is Funday, when you post some comedic content; or Wednesday is Hump Day and you include some uplifting tips to get you through the rest of the week; and perhaps Friday is Fri-Yay!, leading into the weekend with interesting ways to kick back, relax, and unwind. Pay attention to the feedback in the comment section to learn what kind of videos your followers enjoy most. Beyond that, use your other social media to promote your channel—tease it on Instagram, Twitter, and Snapchat. Get the word out and don't be afraid to promote yourself. That should help you spread the word that you're one to watch!

What outfit should I wear to make a musical.ly?
Wear whatever you like, as long as it feels comfortable and true to you. There are days I literally roll out of bed in my sweats with my hair a mess and no makeup and I shoot a video. And there are times I feel like wearing a specific outfit and take time to get ready. Just don't try to be someone you're not—the camera picks up on it, and so will the people who are watching you. It isn't about making a fashion statement, so don't feel any pressure to dress up.

I want to create my own YouTube channel—how do I get started?

This may sound oversimplified, but I say, just start. No excuses. I think what sometimes holds us back is this feeling that you need the highest quality of everything in order to become successful. For instance, stop saying, "I need a better camera before I start making videos." Just use your phone. Don't wait for a special event, a new camera, or fancy lights. If you're inspired to start a YouTube channel, all it takes is you and your phone and some imagination. First ask yourself, "What do I want to share?" There is an endless array of topics you can choose from: comedy, skits, makeup, cooking, crafting, sports, fitness. Start recording what you connect to. Do you want to share your love of fashion? Start sewing. Do you love baking? Make cookies! If you want to make a vlog, then make a vlog. See how it feels and where it takes you. I knew I loved telling stories, so I just put it out there one day. I had no idea if anyone would like it, but it felt true to who I was. My dad always says, "Nothing ventured, nothing gained," and he's right. Start by starting.

When did you first realize you were famous?
I think the first time it kinda hit me, I was taking off on musical.ly and I was in Walmart with my parents. Some girl snapped my photo on her phone. I was in my pj's at the time, and my hair was lookin' like a disaster, and I found

the photo later on Instagram. It went viral! It was surreal. Then there have been times when I'm in an airport or a bookstore and I spot myself on a teen magazine and I'm like, "Wait a sec! That's me!" But I don't think of myself as famous. That's just too weird. I feel like I have this huge fan-mily and we love and support each other, and that's given me a platform to say and do what I love and feel is important. But being "famous" was never the goal and it never will be. I don't want to be anything other than myself.

RED is the color of love, relationships, passion—
it's a bold color, which is why giving your heart
to someone takes guts.

Boys, boys, boys

I've always been boy crazy—even in preschool. There was this cute kid named Sam who had blond hair, blue eyes, and a mischievous grin. At four years old, you don't really ask someone out; it was more like we both blurted, "I like you!" and instantly agreed we were a couple. I remember Sam asked me to the movies and his dad took us. Then he brought me a gift: he wrapped a rock in tissue paper and placed it inside a Brighton heart box. It was only a rock, but the Brighton tin was so pretty, and I cherished it. Our parents thought the whole thing was adorable. It went on for a while, well, through preschool. In pre-K, we would walk down the hallway holding hands, and everyone would whisper about us. But eventually, we went to different elementary schools and things just sort of faded away. There was no drama, and we're still friends who see each other occasionally. The magic is gone, but we'll always have pre-K. . . .

As I got older, I realized relationships are not as simple as my preschool romance. Sam let me off easy and vice versa. Since then, I've had a few relationships that didn't end as smoothly. But dating each of these boys taught me a lot about myself, about love, and about what I really want in a relationship.

The first guy I dated was Zach Clayton. I met Zach when I was fourteen. He was already getting well-known on a live-streaming app and I was just getting known on musical.ly. A manager who was working with him asked me to be a special guest at a meet and greet he was having in Miami with his group, 5Quad. I showed up and immediately it was puppy love between us. All of a sudden it felt like the whole world was trying to pair us up. It became major gossip: *Are they dating? Are they together? Are they a couple?* The ship name "Zariel" became a thing by the end of the weekend! There were Twitter wars from Zach's fans about whether I was worthy of him! The truth is, I really *did* like him and he really *did* like me. After that meet and greet, we all went back to a house they'd rented and went swimming, zoomed around on their hoverboards, made musical.lys, and played fun games all night long. That was the beginning of this tender, sweet friendship that always felt like it was bubbling under the surface and kind of hoping for something more. We would have these funny, cute, flirty conversations tiptoeing around the idea of actually dating because neither one of us felt confident enough to step up and say it.

Later that year, Arii (one of my longtime best friends) and I got an invite from Zach's manager to join Zach and 5Quad at DigiFest in Texas as their special guests. I'd never been so excited in my life. DigiFest was a huge dream of mine and getting to do it with Zach was more than I could have hoped for. I remember in the airport, Arii and I didn't know what we'd do when we got onstage, but we didn't even care. For me, getting to hang out with Zach and be at DigiFest was enough. After our first show, my parents let us hang out at the hotel—just Arii, me, Zach, and 5Quad. One thing about my parents that I've always appreciated is that they have always trusted me to make good choices. But maybe in this case, it wasn't the best idea. Not because I did anything bad, but, well, let me explain. . . .

We all went out to eat and then back to the hotel. After a while, Nick, Edwin, Timmy, and Rudan (Zach's friends from 5Quad) went back to their rooms and Arii, Zach, and I were hanging out by ourselves. So what else would a few teenagers do? Play hide-and-seek of course! There I was, behind the door hiding from Arii, when all of a sudden, Zach came up from behind and smacked me in the back of my head with his pillow. My mouth crashed into the door and I cracked my front tooth in half! I remember panicking and thinking to myself, "Oh my gosh! What am I going to do?!? We're a thousand miles from home, about to do a show tomorrow, and my tooth is chipped in half! How am I going to explain this to my parents?" I ended up telling my parents the truth that night and they were super cool about it. But what I remember most was how kind and concerned Zach was. He was practically crying about how bad he felt. That's something about Zach I'll always love and appreciate: he has a heart of gold and genuinely cares more about others than he does for himself. That next day, I did a live stream about how my tooth was chipped and how important it is to embrace yourself, flaws and all. I remember thinking it was really important to show my supporters that you won't always look your best and feel your best, but that you should always accept yourself the way you are. And I believed that with all my heart. But full disclosure: the story I told about how it happened wasn't true. Zach and I weren't dating yet and I didn't want him to get hate, so I kinda, sorta left out the part where he hit me with the pillow. But even with my entire tooth trauma, something good came out of it. I realized that Zach and I really did like each other—and I think that scared both of us.

For a few months, things were a little awkward between us. We lived in different states, didn't see each other, and couldn't figure out if we were just friends or more. And I think we were afraid to be really honest with each other about how we were feeling. But the pressure for "Zariel" on social media was getting really intense. It was like the whole Twitter and Instagram universe wanted something for us that possibly we didn't really want for ourselves or weren't ready for. A few months later, we finally met up again at Playlist Orlando. I was so happy to see him, and that weekend, I think from all of the pressure, we kind of caved and said, "Okay, maybe we are a couple."

We dated for two months before we realized it wasn't the smartest decision. Looking back on it now, it all felt very rushed; our relationship didn't have a chance to evolve on its own. There was so much pressure to post videos together and tweet about each other and take selfies together that it never had a chance to be real. It felt like we were always trying to please everyone else instead of really getting to know each other. It was a little like living in a fishbowl, too; everywhere we went we were scrutinized and it was hard to just be us. I really cared for him, but we were both young and inexperienced and got swept up in all that public pressure. It felt more like we were playing the roles of Boyfriend/Girlfriend rather than really living the parts. It's okay; Zach and I are still super-good friends because we never actually had a falling-out. We're just two people who are very real, and we realized that wasn't the case with what was going on between us. It didn't feel genuine; it felt forced, and to make matters worse, even though we were both uncomfortable with how things were going, neither of us would talk about it. We didn't talk about things in the beginning when we were figuring out our feelings. We didn't talk about the pressure to start dating. And we didn't talk about how uncomfortable things got once we did date. Lesson learned: you can't expect to have a good relationship if you can't communicate.

Eventually, we both decided we were better off keeping things in the friendship zone, and now we are actually closer than we have ever been! Honestly, it feels much better without the expectations or the speculation in the magazines. We can just be ourselves and enjoy each other's company sans drama. If I had to post our relationship status on social media, I would probably say "it's *not* complicated anymore" and we're both much happier because of it.

After a breakup, it's pretty normal to get a little skittish about the next relationship that comes along. I certainly didn't want to make the same mistakes. That's the place I was in when my next boyfriend came into the picture. I felt like I needed to be sure and not rush things, so I put up a lot of walls and defenses before I let him in. Even though there's no hate between us now, he deserves respect and I thought it best to keep his name private.

I was fifteen at the time, and I really felt myself falling in a way I never had before. I remember thinking when we started dating, "If we ever break up, this is *really* gonna hurt." Of course, it did, and of course, I'm going to tell you about it.

But let's start at the beginning. Boyfriend #2 is who I count as my first real relationship. I cared deeply for him, and we were together for nine months, which felt like a lifetime. We knew each other a while from the world of social media and hanging out with the same friend group. I remember thinking, "This boy is seriously cute," but all we had for a while was a friendship and the occasional flirtation. Then, one day, he DM'd me on Twitter: "Hey what's your number?" I gave it to him and we started texting and FaceTiming and I slowly let him into my life. For me, when I open those doors, it means a lot. I'm not someone who trusts easily, and I need to really feel very comfortable and close to someone before letting my guard down. As all of this was growing between us, we found out we were both going to be on the same tour together for a whole month. I was so excited; I couldn't imagine anything more perfect.

We wound up in rehearsals in LA and that's where we started spending time one-on-one and dating. On the tour, we traveled the country together, and all of a sudden, it felt very intense. We were literally together all the time, joined at the hip, finishing each other's sentences, laughing at each other's jokes. It was like being married because we were always together, which, let's face it, is not reality. It was this little perfect dream of a relationship. Perhaps, it was a little too perfect. While we were on tour, we spent all our time together and didn't let anyone else in. My friends started telling me that I was isolating myself and that I wasn't there for them as much anymore. Looking back, they were right. I was giving him all my energy and was ignoring my closest friends. They tried to tell me that I was alienating them and that they were concerned about me. I put up my defenses and pushed them away, feeling that maybe they were just jealous of my relationship. And that should have been a red flag. Even in the best relationships, there should always be room for your friends and family, especially if you realize that they love you and always want the best for you. But I didn't see that at the time. The only thing I wanted was to enjoy my time with my boyfriend as long as I could. And while we were on tour together, in our perfect little bubble, things were fun, silly, and we thought, "real."

We both knew that little bubble would eventually have to burst, and of course, when the tour came to an end, it did. We went home to different states, and while our parents were open to us traveling back and forth to see each other, let's be honest: the long-distance thing sucks. We continued making videos and musical.lys together; we did photo shoots and supported each other a lot. But then, as time progressed, the flaws in our relationship started showing themselves to us. Without the protection of the tour-life bubble, our relationship started falling apart. In reality, it was probably already falling apart before then.

He went on another tour, this one without me. During the time he was away, things began to change. He was doing his thing on a tour bus with a lot of other people and I was busy working on my music and acting projects. With both of us in different time zones and on conflicting schedules, it became harder and harder to FaceTime. Often when I would call, he was onstage or in a meet and greet and when he tried to connect with me, I was busy in the studio or on set. Not only was the lack of communication an issue, but our talks were also sometimes strained. I started to realize that maybe we didn't have a lot to talk about or that maybe we didn't have much in common. So we had started having conversations that felt forced instead of real. There was a growing unease and I started feeling stressed all the time.

There was also a new rift in our bond. I am not a jealous person by nature, but I found myself getting more and more insecure. I wasn't able to talk with him or spend time with him like before, but I could still see pictures on his Snapchat with all these other people having fun. I totally understand that it went both ways: he was able to get a glimpse into my life through my social media and see my adventures without him. Then one day some random girl DM'd me on my finsta: "Oh, I saw your boyfriend and he's really cute." She was at his show, and she had posted several selfies with him. All the feelings of stress and lack of communication and insecurity blew up in me and I freaked.

When I finally got through to him on the phone, he thought I was completely crazy: "Why would you feel insecure about a picture? It wasn't like that at all." And I'm sure it wasn't. But that was the thing—I didn't know what it was like. I wasn't there with him and I missed that. I missed the closeness and the security I had when we were together. When we were apart, my mind was filled with doubt. And when we were able to talk, it started to feel like all we ever did end up talking about were the problems and stress we were each feeling. We both seemed to be questioning each other more and more about who we were with, what we were doing, and why we were even together.

When he came home, things were briefly better. For a little while, we were able to recapture those feelings we'd had from our tour. Then slowly but surely, the same insecurities that had begun when we were apart started showing up in person. And the sense that we really didn't have a lot in common became very real. We fought a lot to the point where that was all we ever did. Our relationship was coming apart at the seams: we were not actually breaking up—we were just *fighting*. On top of it all, I had alienated my friends so much and had done such a good job of telling myself and them that our relationship was perfect, that I felt I couldn't even admit how much we were struggling. I felt so alone. Then, one day, we got into this really bad argument, and he said, "That's it. We're done."

I was in disbelief. I thought to myself, "Wait—that's not how it works! You owe me more than that. This can't just end like this, can it?" We ended up FaceTiming later that day, and texting the next, trying to hash out the hurt and disappointment on both sides. It was weird; we couldn't let it go. We went around and around in circles, yelling, crying, trying to point blame and at the same time fix things that were too broken to fix. It took a few days but the relationship did come to an end. I finally said enough is enough, and as much as it was tearing me apart to do so, I knew it was the right decision. That's the big lesson I learned from this whole heart-wrenching experience: when a relationship is toxic, the time must come for you to let it go. You have to respect yourself and know that you're worth more.

I see now that I was desperate to make things work, to keep it going, and I didn't realize I was compromising who I was. I thought that if we broke up, my life would be over—it felt that all-consuming. Well, fast-forward now a few months: I lived. I got over it. I moved on. And he has, too. I wouldn't say it was fun to go through, but it was enlightening to say the least. I learned a lot about what I want and what I don't want in a relationship. Right at this moment, I'm not sure I want a boyfriend at all—and I'm okay with that. There was a time when I was in school and I thought having a boyfriend was the be-all, end-all. But now, I'm not in a rush. I think I have a lot of things I want to do before I dive in again. I need to be happy 110 percent with the person I am, confident, secure, and loving myself before I'm prepared to love someone else.

And I'm working on all of the above! That said, if I find someone who complements me, someone I really feel a connection to, then maybe it will happen. But I'm not going to be a contestant on *The Bachelor* any time soon, and I'm not in the market for a relationship; I think I prefer to let it find me rather than go searching high and low for it. I have awesome friends, an amazing family, and that's a lot of love in my corner.

Which is a good thing, because when you break up, you need all the support you can get. You need to mourn, then pick yourself up and move on. The temptation of course is to say, "Oh, no, I'm not going through this again." But you do and you will until you find that one perfect person for you. Each time you get a little closer and you learn more about yourself in the process. My parents actually met each other when they were fifteen and started dating when they were sixteen. The fact that they're still together has always given me such a deep belief in love. I know it's out there.

Baby Steps

10 SIMPLE WAYS TO KNOW
IF HE'S INTO YOU

Guys aren't that tough to figure out. They all basically have the same moves (no offense . . .) when it comes to sending signals. (Note: I'm using "he" here, but this advice applies to girls and boys, gay and straight and in-between!)

1. **He finds a reason to talk to you, even if it's a totally lame reason.** Like, "Hey, do you think it's gonna snow today?" when there isn't a cloud in the sky and it's seventy degrees.

2. **His name keeps coming up.** Maybe it's because he's asked one of your friends you know and trust to whisper in your ear, "Isn't Tyler cute/hot/smart/so nice?" Wonder how much he had to pay them . . .

3. **He catches your eye from across the room.**
   Seriously, he is always staring in your direction!
   Either you have spinach stuck in your teeth or
   he's fixated on your face.

4. **He finds a reason to get physical,** i.e.,
   accidentally touching your hand as he passes
   back a homework assignment in class or brushing
   against you as he hurries by to homeroom.

5. **He teases you—but it's all in good fun.** He
   isn't really making fun of your milk mustache in
   the cafeteria—he actually digs female facial hair.

6. **He asks for help on a math problem, a
   Spanish assignment, his English essay.** Any
   reason he can think of to spend one-on-one time
   with you.

7. **He pays close attention to small details
   about you**—how else would he know to bring
   you an iced vanilla latte with skim milk and an
   extra shot of espresso topped with whipped cream
   on your birthday?

8. **He DMs, Snaps, or texts you out of the blue for no reason.** Sometimes it's a single word ("Hey") or a wink emoji, just to let you know you're on his mind.

9. **He tries to impress you.** Whenever you're in class, he raises his hand in an effort to wow you with his academic genius. It would be even more impressive if the teacher called on him.

And finally, the sure sign that the boy's got it bad: he gets all hot and bothered whenever you look at him/talk to him. His cheeks literally flush stop-sign red and he can't help stammering or looking at his feet. The more tongue-tied he is in your presence, the bigger the chance that he's not just socially awkward or shy; he's really, truly, deeply, madly crushing on you.

#askariel

I literally cannot stop obsessing over this kid in my math class. How do I get him to notice me?

Start by making small talk: "Hey, do you understand this homework question?" or "Can I borrow your class notes from yesterday?" You want to take things slow and keep it light and as obsess-less as possible or you'll scare him off. You need to be comfortable just chatting with him before you can take it to the next level. When you think you're there, then you can casually ask, "Do you want to go to a movie Friday?" Don't infer that it's anything more than two friends just hanging out, because at this point, that's all it is. The best advice I can give you from personal experience is go slow, take your time, gauge how he reacts when you talk to him. At this point, I seriously turn into a *Criminal Minds* profiler and look for ANY clues as to whether he likes me or not. If he keeps things short and sweet and doesn't seem interested, you may have to acknowledge that this could be one-sided. And that's okay. My mom will cheerfully remind me that he's not the only boy out there. If the object of your obsession isn't responding, then maybe it's time to find someone who can appreciate you for who you are.

My BF says I'm "smothering" him. He says I call and text him too much, but I can't help it. How much do you think is too much?

I would say that depends on both people in the relationship, but 24/7 is probably a good measure of going to extremes. It also depends on how close or far you live. If the guy is your next-door neighbor and you're constantly texting and calling, I'd say you need to take it down a notch. If he lives across the country and you miss him, then Skyping or FaceTiming a few times a day to feel connected is probably more acceptable. You have to figure out what feels comfortable for both of you and have an open and honest talk about it. If he's telling you it's too much, then listen and respect his feelings. At the end of the day, you guys are individuals and you both need space to do your own thing and be your own person. Sometimes I think giving someone space actually helps you get closer. It shows you trust each other, and that's what will make a relationship work.

I broke up with this guy and I found out he just asked out one of my best friends and she said yes. I'm so pissed at both of them! What should I do?

Ouch, I've been through this one, too. Don't ya worry. Here's the facts: you already broke up with this boy, which means he's clearly not right for you. So you move on from that. To me, this is really a question about your "friend." If she started dating your ex without talking to you about it first, that, in my mind, is a clear violation of the girl code. When it happened to me, my biggest problem was the fact that I wasn't spoken to before they were already dating. To me that was disrespectful of our friendship and my feelings and extremely hurtful. If your friend is a good friend, she would make sure you were cool with it. The fact that she didn't? Well, actions speak louder than words.

The deets on dating

Let's face it, asking someone out is scary. Historically, guys have always done the asking, but times are changing and so are the rules. We live in a time when girls should feel empowered to make the first move. For the record, I am not a girl who feels particularly confident about asking a guy out. Which isn't to say I would never make the first move—I'm just not going to go into it blindly. I'm not going to be clueless as to whether he likes me or not. I'm not the type to walk up to a boy I haven't spoken to and all of a sudden say, "Hey let's go on a date!" I will give hints, feel it out, bounce it off his friends, and then, if I truly feel there's a strong possibility that he's into me, I might ask him out in a very casual way: "Why don't we catch a movie?" No expectations, no stress, just easy, breezy, two friends hanging out, catching the new *Star Wars*. Then you see where it goes from there.

We all have a fear of rejection, especially if you've had a crush on someone for a while and have built up the moment in your head. I have to remind myself sometimes that guys are no different than us girls. Just because traditionally guys have done the asking doesn't mean it's easier for them. They feel the pressure, too. So, I guess my advice for all of us is to remember it doesn't have to be that way; we're overcomplicating things. Ask someone out because you simply want to get to know them or think they are someone it would be fun to spend some time with. Some of my best dates were super casual and just a good excuse to learn more about each other and see how we connected. I've never really been "taken out" on a date, where you get all dressed up and there's candlelight and violins playing. I've had friendships that evolved into dating, so we skipped a lot of the formalities. To be honest, one of my best dates ever with Ex-BF #2 was in New York City surrounded by mobs of people in Times Square. It was anything but quiet and intimate—but we had the most amazing time. We had dinner at the Hard Rock Cafe, which is a great choice, because it's a meal and a rock-'n'-roll museum in one. We walked around checking out all the guitars, photographs, and memorabilia, picking out our favorites. Afterward we went outside and strolled under all the crazy, bright neon signs and video billboards, taking in the pulse of the city and the people. It was pretty wonderful: a loud, frenzied, taxi-horns-honking kind of wonderful. We wound up at the M&M store, where we designed our own candies in pink and blue with our names on them. I remember we talked a lot about anything and everything that night, and I didn't for one second feel like I had to pretend to be someone I wasn't. That, to me, is the sign of a great date: the conversation flows effortlessly, and both of you are simply being who you are without any pretenses or trying too hard to impress. I made silly jokes and said whatever came to my mind without worrying that he would think I was weird or goofy.

Not every date you go on will go this well. Some will totally tank and that goes with the territory. My mom always reminds me that everyone's journey is different and you may have to kiss some frogs until you find your prince. I'm lucky—I haven't had a major date disaster. I've never humiliated myself or watched the clock, counting the minutes and wishing it would be over. If you've experienced one of the above scenarios, try not to stress over it; it happens to everyone at some point. It's better you know now rather than later so you can spare yourself some heartache. Some dates aren't total disasters, more like puzzles you can't quite piece together. They leave you scratching your head and wondering. In that case, it may be too soon to tell. You might need to go out a few more times to figure it out. But eventually, you have to reach a comfort level: a good relationship starts with being 100 percent comfortable being yourself around this person. I can't be walking on eggshells when we're together. If I'm going to be in a relationship, it has to be real and it has to be relaxed.

You're not going to click with everyone you go out with. Sometimes the rapport is instantaneous; other times, not so much. First dates are usually the hardest because there are lots of nerves and you want to make a good first impression. You don't want to embarrass yourself by saying or doing the wrong thing. You don't want to have lipstick smeared across your face or sit there, staring at each other, saying nothing. Those long silences are the worst! I always feel like I have to do something, *anything* to break the ice. I'm good at conversation and asking questions, but occasionally, even I blank, especially if I'm nervous. That's when I resort to my preplanned list of backup questions. I like to ask about family: "How many siblings do you have?" "Do you guys get along?" "What do your parents do?" I love movies, so I might ask, "What's your favorite movie and how many times have you seen it?" or "What's the last really great movie you saw?" Be observant: if the person you like wears a jersey of their favorite sports team, you can't go wrong asking them about it. I might say, "So, do you like basketball?" "Who is your favorite team?" Or "Do you play any sports?" Or talk about travel: "What's the coolest place you've ever been?" "Where are you dying to go on a vacation?" When you ask questions, you're showing the other person that you are truly interested in what they think and that you want to get to know them on a deeper level.

My parents have always taught me to listen carefully to what people say. Pay attention to the responses—it can lead to a really great conversation and discovering how much you two have in common (or not!). I'm someone who believes no topic should be off-limits. Whatever comes up is okay to talk about. I think if you start the relationship off with honesty, then that becomes your foundation. I also don't think there are any set rules for dating except for one: no phones! If I'm talking and trying to get to know you and you're checking Snapchat or texting friends, I'm going to be like, "Hello? Am I interrupting you?" It's sad but sometimes I feel like our generation only feels comfortable communicating by text, over FaceTime, or on other apps.

We don't know how to just *be* with each other in the same room and talk, and that's what can make dating and spending time with someone face-to-face feel so strange and awkward. I know when a guy I'm crushing on sends me a text, I take the time to formulate the perfect response. One reply can take me ten minutes because I have to run it by my friends and opinion shop. But you can't do that on a date; the response has to be in the moment. You're on your own—you can't text your BFF, "What do I say now?" or tell your date, "Can you give me a few minutes to get back to you on that?" Say what's in your heart and in your head if you want him to do the same. Simple, right?

Story Time

MY "BLINDSIDE" CRUSH

Here's the backstory: I had just broken up with my last boyfriend and was on a roller coaster of emotions. One day, I'd be super happy and excited about my future; the next day, I would wake up feeling like my life was over and I was certain I'd be single forever! And that's when it happened. On one particularly sad day, my friends had had enough of me wallowing in self-pity and told me to get up, get dressed, and get ready to go out. I followed their instructions, grudgingly at first, but as I started getting ready and putting on some makeup and a cute outfit, I began feeling more optimistic than I had been for a while. On a side note, sometimes when you are feeling down, doing something out of your norm can lift your spirits quickly. In this case, I have my friends to thank for that!

Anyhow, after I had gotten myself dolled up and feelin' pretty freakin' cute, my friends took me to one of our favorite hangout spots. I thought it was just going to be the four of us, but waiting at a larger table was a group of three boys who called us over. At first I didn't recognize them, but soon realized they were mutual friends I'd met on a couple of occasions, at parties and at friends' houses. Before I even had a chance to sit down with them, I excused myself to use the bathroom. When I came back, my friend Arii got up and scooted me into the booth to sit next to my future crush. At the time, it didn't even occur to me why she didn't just stay seated and let me sit at the end, but as this guy and I started talking, I caught a glimpse at Arii's smirk, and that's when ya girl KNEW she was scheming. She had definitely planned this! Throughout the evening I started to get those butterflies in my stomach and felt myself smiling endlessly. The funny thing about this whole situation? I had never really noticed him before. I mean, he was cute and all, but because I was in another relationship I never looked at him like that. But now, sitting next to him and talking and getting to know him, I was completely blindsided by an instant attraction and chemistry. This crush never really amounted to anything; it kind of blossomed and fizzled out within a few weeks (for the record, we're still great friends and we both agree that's the way it should be). But it served a greater purpose: it got me out of my slump and made me realize that I could—and should—look for love again.

Baby Steps

HOW TO TALK YOUR PARENTS INTO LETTING YOU DATE

My parents know me better than anyone else, and I've always really valued their opinions. They love me and they want the best for me, so when something or someone doesn't sit right with them, I listen up. Does that mean we always see eye to eye? Of course not. I know a lot of parents and teenagers butt heads when it comes to dating. With the boy I like now, I'm lucky; he's my best friend and he's been to our house a million times so my parents know him and like him and would have no issue with me dating him (thank god). In fact, my mom has said to us, "Can you guys just date already? Please, please, please?" But if your mom and dad aren't ready for you to start a relationship, you've got some convincing to do:

Wait till there's someone in the picture. If your parents have a strict "no dating till you're older" policy, don't—I repeat, don't—argue with them until you need to. Wait until you have someone you're interested in (and who's interested in you back) before you try to negotiate terms. It's not worth fighting over a hypothetical. Choose your battles wisely.

Break it to them . . . slowly. If you're feeling strongly about someone and want your parents' blessing, I would start by saying, "So there's this cute boy . . ." rather than "I'm in love with this guy . . ." Give them a chance to make peace with the fact that their little kid is having some pretty adult emotions and warm to the idea. Keep the communication open between you but spare them the stuff you would tell your BFF, like how you dream about kissing him and can't think of anything else besides his two perfect lips. No parent wants to hear that.

Talk him up. With my parents, I have always warmed them up to a new boyfriend by convincing them he's a really good person. Always emphasize the positives: "So did I tell you that he got an A on his math test? Did I mention he's president of the student council? Did you know he volunteers at an animal shelter?" You get the point—paint him in the best light possible so they agree he's good enough for you. On the flip side, if he isn't such a great guy and you can't honestly think of anything wonderful to say about him, maybe it's time to reevaluate what you see in him to begin with. Trust me, you don't want to get hurt.

Ask them why they feel the way they do. I promise you, they have a good reason. Maybe they're worried you'll get hurt, and they're trying to protect you. Maybe they think a boyfriend will distract you from your schoolwork. They may see something you don't; hear them out and let them know you understand and respect their feelings. They love you and they care—so cut them some slack.

Prove that you're mature enough to handle it. That means sticking to their rules whenever and wherever possible: obeying curfews, getting good grades, cleaning your room without being told. The more you show them how responsible you are, the more they will ease up.

Don't sneak around behind their backs. This one goes without saying. It will only make matters worse because when you get caught (notice how I said *when* not *if*), they will never trust you again. Not to mention, though unlikely, it could be very dangerous if something bad happens and your parents have no idea where you are or who you're with.

If the answer is still no, you have options. I know it might not be exactly what you want, but there's nothing wrong with you being friends with a guy for a while—it will only make your relationship stronger. Ask him to come over when your parents are home so they get to know him (and you get to spend time with him); suggest your mom or dad drive you guys to a movie and pick you up after so they're not worrying about your whereabouts. Or instead of a solo date, go out in a group of friends—that often feels a lot less scary to a parent because there's safety in numbers. Just be patient, and try to resist the urge to scream, cry, whine, or slam your bedroom door. Your parents aren't the bad guys; they're just a little overprotective. If they're like mine, they're also right most of the time.

#AskAriel

I'm going out for the first time with this guy I really like and I don't know what I should wear. Help!

The first thing you need to know is where you're going. Out to a nice dinner? A movie? Bowling? It makes a huge difference in how you dress. Do your homework; look the place up online and check out some pictures of guests there so you can gauge how fancy (or not) it is. In general, I think you have to find a balance: when it comes to date dressing, you don't want to be too "extra," but then again, you don't want to be too basic either. I'd say my go-to date night look is jeans, a nice shirt, maybe a little jacket or sweater if we're going somewhere that has air-conditioning. You want to always wear something that makes you feel both comfy and confident. Stick to your style and don't second-guess yourself. He's either gonna love it or not, and frankly, if he doesn't, then he's not the guy for you. If I went out with a boy who didn't like my long nails or my hoop earrings, I'd know he's not the one. If he's right for you, he will respect your style and think you're beautiful inside and out no matter what outfit you pick.

This guy asked me out and I don't really like him. How do I turn him down?

I've been in this situation before, and you need to do it as kindly and gently as possible to spare this kid's feelings. Think about how you would like someone to respond if this was you who was asking someone out—the ol' "do unto others." You wouldn't want to hear "Ugh, get away from me! I don't like you." Instead, let him down easy: "Oh, that's so nice of you, but I can't, I'm sorry . . ." If he still doesn't take the hint, you could try: "Aw, that's so nice of you. But I'm really not looking for a relationship at the moment. Can we just be friends?" When someone puts their heart out there, try your very best not to trample it.

I feel like ever since my BFF started dating this kid, she has no time for me. Does having a boyfriend mean you just dump your friends?

No, it does not. But it's also complicated. I've been on both sides of this scenario, feeling dumped and doing the dumping. I honestly didn't mean to push my friends away;

I was just so infatuated at the time, he was all I could think about, and I thought my friends were super, super happy for me. That's what happens when you're on cloud nine: nothing else matters. My friends literally had to stage an intervention: "Hey, Ariel, you're so obsessed with this kid, don't forget about us!" I immediately apologized for being so clueless and made plans to spend more time with them. I think you should talk to your BFF because chances are, she's unaware, too. Be honest with how you feel and if she's a good friend, she will fix it.

What are your favorite love songs to listen to?
I have a really, really long list of songs that put me in my feelings. Julia Michaels's "Issues" and "Heaven" for starters. Recently, my friend Daniel Skye told me about "2:AM" by Anthony Russo and I've been listening to it nonstop, it's so good! Any Daniel Caesar song, although I'm partial to "Best Part" and "Get You." Old Taylor Swift for sure, anything Bieber, H.E.R., SZA's "Love Galore" and "Supermodel," Bryson Tiller, Madison Beer. Oh, my gosh, I could go on and on. Put some Baby Ariel in there, too—she'll definitely put you in your feelings!

 I broke up with my high school boyfriend in the fall— we're seniors and we were dating since tenth grade.

The prom is a month away and neither of us has a date. Should I ask him?

Wow, that could be really tricky. I think it depends. Are you guys still cool? Are you friends now even though you're broken up? And would it send the wrong signals (like might he think that you want to get back together with him even if you don't)? And will people who might be interested in you (or him) now think that you're not available? You have to consider some of those things first. If you are both totally cool and on the same page, then go for it.

I caught my boyfriend texting another girl. When I asked him what was going on he said nothing, but my gut is telling me it's something. What should I do?

Trust is one of the most important things you can have in a relationship and it's so important to trust your instincts. If you don't trust him, or if you're insecure about your relationship, then that might be a bigger problem than just him texting another girl. When I started to lose trust, that's when my relationship fell apart. Your BF's texting could be totally innocent . . . or not. But the point here is that you are questioning his loyalty and something is gnawing away at you and making you feel uncomfortable. You need to have a sit-down conversation. Tell him how you feel, that it's bothering you and causing you to have doubts, and that you want to be completely honest and open with him and expect the same in return. If he still insists he's being true to you, then it's time to make a choice: either you believe him and continue on with the relationship without jealousy, or you don't and end the relationship. It's not healthy for either of you to stay in a situation that makes you feel uncomfortable.

ORANGE *is the color of creativity—mix energy (yellow) and passion (red) and you've got a perfect formula for success.*

I'm never bored

My mind is working 24/7—it's probably the reason I end up drinking way too much coffee (about five cups a day!) and staying up way too late at night. I'm either dealing with something in the present or planning for the future, and I really don't know how to 100 percent shut down unless I'm sleeping. And even then, I'm dreaming of possibilities . . .

. . . and I have no time to waste just dreaming them. I need to put them into action. I definitely get some of this mentality from my mom; she is the boredom buster in our family. She's constantly on the go, and when I was little, I seriously thought she was Super Mom (still do!). Just recently, we were on this looooooong car trip, and my brother and I were in the back seat, basically staring alternately at our phones and into space, yawning and trying to get comfy in our SUV. His dirty socks were in my face, my playlist kept glitching, and I couldn't deal with the fact that I had five more hours of this to look forward to. That's when Mom piped up from the front, "Let's play a game!" You should know that my mom always means business; there's no zoning out on your phone with her. She's the master of coming up with games to get us all engaged: Guess This Person, Name That Tune, and, my all-time fave, Last Letter. She'll start with a topic—say, "food"—and each person has to use the last letter to think of another word. For example, let's say I start the game with "duck." Then Jacob would have to take the letter "k" and he might say "kiwi." Dad is up next: he has to take the last letter in "kiwi," "i" and come up with a food—like "ice cream" or "iceberg lettuce." We keep going, and the answers get progressively sillier. Then we move on to another category. It's fun, and it does get us all connected and communicating as a family. Which is a big improvement over silence and stinky feet.

Besides always having places to be and things to do, I have a purpose that motivates me: I want to keep learning, growing, and challenging myself to discover my next big thing. I want to do great things—not just mediocre ones—

and I want to make a difference. I think that's the key: you'll never be bored if you have a goal you're striving to achieve. Sometimes my friends complain they have nothing to do, and I'm like, "Well, whose fault is that? Get off your butt!" It's never too early to start dreaming about your future and setting the wheels in motion. It's never too soon to make your move.

Having a goal in mind is your first step to making something happen. If you know the direction and where you want to wind up, it's okay if you don't know exactly how to get there. Your intention might be "I want to have my own YouTube channel" or "I want to write a novel." I love goal setting because it lets me take control of my life and zoom in on what's most important to me. As a teenager, it's easy to get swept up in day-to-day drama and lose focus. We've got homework, social lives, family responsibilities, extracurriculars—the list goes on and on. I jot my goals down in my journal or on my phone (*Perform to sold-out stadiums. Win a Grammy award. Write and direct my own movie.*) so I don't ever lose sight of what I want to be doing and achieving amid all the hustle and bustle and chaos. I make a whole lot of lists, and I'm also a visual person. I respond to pictures because they help me see it—which helps me be it. If you're the same way, you can make yourself a mood board or a Pinterest board to get your creativity flowing—choose pictures or quotes that speak to you and inspire you. (More on my own dream board super-duper soon!) The important thing is to set this all up as little reminders for yourself whenever you're feeling uninspired or overwhelmed. I even collected a bunch of images when I was preparing to write this book, and they helped me envision the flow of the chapters and the different topics I wanted to talk about in each.

Some people might say, "Why create any extra work for myself? I already have enough essays and tests and papers." I hear you, but you should never think of your dreams as chores. They need to be nurtured. Success takes work—A LOT of work—and you have to be focused and driven toward your goals. You can't be lazy. I know it sounds like the ideal life: have fun and rack up followers. But I am constantly working, planning, preparing, traveling . . . and worrying I won't get it all done. I'm all for vacations and the occasional spa day, but I feel bad if I'm being lazy or procrastinating because I know I'm not being my most productive self. Yeah, it's great to sleep in till noon, but then I think, "What could I have done in this amount of time I totally threw away? Made a video? Written some song lyrics? Did some journaling?" You see my point? There's so much out there just waiting for you to seize it. Never let your life fall into snooze mode.

Dream Board

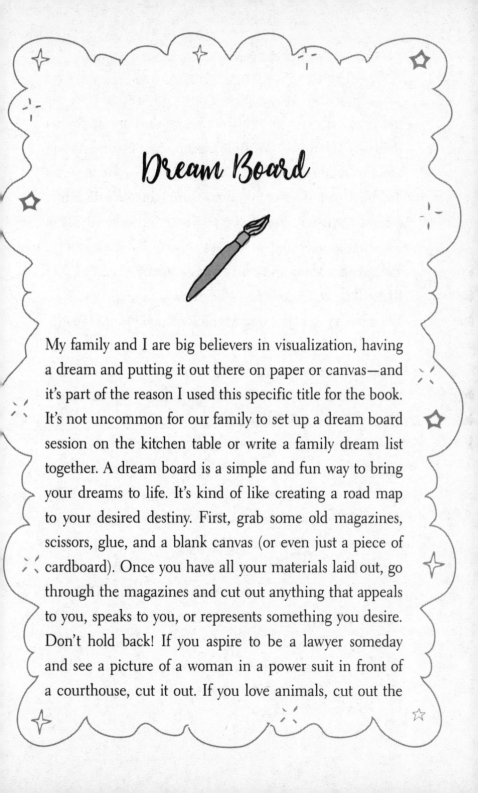

My family and I are big believers in visualization, having a dream and putting it out there on paper or canvas—and it's part of the reason I used this specific title for the book. It's not uncommon for our family to set up a dream board session on the kitchen table or write a family dream list together. A dream board is a simple and fun way to bring your dreams to life. It's kind of like creating a road map to your desired destiny. First, grab some old magazines, scissors, glue, and a blank canvas (or even just a piece of cardboard). Once you have all your materials laid out, go through the magazines and cut out anything that appeals to you, speaks to you, or represents something you desire. Don't hold back! If you aspire to be a lawyer someday and see a picture of a woman in a power suit in front of a courthouse, cut it out. If you love animals, cut out the picture of those cute puppies. If you want to be an actor, rip the page with an image of an Oscar award out. It doesn't matter if you're still in middle school, or if these things seem far-fetched as you sit in your room. They represent a dream, a goal. If a word or phrase jumps out and motivates you, cut that out, too. Once you have a generous pile of inspiring images and words, it's time to lay them out on your blank canvas and start to paste them. There are NO RULES here. . . . You can glue, draw in images, write . . . The idea is to create a visual representation of your dreams. Once it's done, put the board in a place you see every day. You'll be surprised that just this simple reminder of what and who and where you want to be in the future will actually help you achieve your goals.

A dream list is the same idea. Get a piece of paper and start writing down all the things you want to do, the places you want to go, and the things you want to achieve. Keep the sentences simple and concise and don't give yourself any limitations. I remember hearing an inspirational story about the actor Jim Carrey before he was successful and was still struggling to make it in the acting world. He wrote himself a ten-million-dollar check and kept it in his wallet, where he would look at it every day. It was a daily reminder of what he wanted to achieve. It may sound silly to some people, but you know what? Jim Carrey went on to exceed ten million, so who's laughing now? About eight years ago, my mom, dad, Jacob, and I sat down and decided to write our own family dream list. We hung it on the refrigerator and it stayed there for some time until it ended up lost in a pile of papers. And then five years later, cleaning out our kitchen junk drawer (doesn't everyone have one of those?), we found the list and were so surprised that we had achieved six out of the ten things we'd written down!

1. we went to Israel and met my extended family,
2. we had a family trip to Panama,
3. we traveled to Paris,
4. we built a pool,
5. we renovated our house, and lastly
6. we took a hot air balloon ride . . . twice!

These were all things we had written down together as a family, and the mere act of putting it out there helped it manifest into reality! As a family we love to organize a yearly adventure and choose a new destination to explore. Our annual family vacations have included places that were just a short drive away and as far away as the Middle East, which required an eighteen-hour flight and a stopover in London! I can't really choose a favorite trip because there are memorable moments that I cherish from each and every one. But I've chosen a few highlights.

North Carolina is definitely a choice destination for us

and we've vacationed there at least a half dozen times. It's a convenient getaway because of how close it is to Florida, and there's a ton of stuff to do there. From hiking to sledding to gem mining, farmers' markets to historic home tours, we are never bored! Ever since we were little, Jacob and I and our cousins, (Alexandra, Connor, and Keira) have played a game when visiting historic homes: we call dibs on our favorite bedrooms based on style and personality and pretend we lived there at the time it was built. So you can imagine how excited we were when we visited the Biltmore Estate, near Asheville, the largest privately owned home in the US, with over thirty bedrooms! We playacted all day and pretended we were the only ones there. That trip was particularly memorable because it was the first time Jacob and I got to experience snow. We had rented a beautiful house in Highlands and on our second night there, while enjoying a family game of Monopoly, we noticed it had begun to flurry. We all started screaming in excitement, put on our coats and boots and mittens over our pajamas, and ran outside. My aunt Yarima made us hot chocolate with marshmallows and we just stared up at the sky and watched the snowfall and drank our hot cocoa. It was a magical night and an all-around enchanting trip!

I have been to Israel a few times, but one of my favorite trips was the year Papa, my grandpa, invited my mom, her sister, and two brothers, including spouses and kids, to Israel for two weeks. My mom's cousin was getting married and Papa decided very generously that it would be amazing for us all to attend and, wow, was it ever! We met an unbelievable amount of extended family and even got to hang out with my great-grandparents, which was extremely special. We visited so many different cities including Jerusalem, where we did a tour of the old city; we stayed in an artist's villa on a vineyard in the mystical city of Tsfat, which had the most incredible views of the Galilee, and got to visit my mom's old stomping grounds in Tel Aviv, where she went to school. We hiked, explored, climbed, ate, laughed, and enjoyed each other's company while taking in Israel's rich history.

Three summers ago we finally made it to my father's birthplace in Panama. This had been a dream destination for quite a while and we wanted to make sure we could go and spend enough time to really explore the country and also meet our huge extended family! It was so wonderful to see and experience the country where my father was born. We were able to visit the Miraflores Locks and cross the Panama Canal and go into the control tower thanks to my aunt Maylin, who works there. We went snorkeling in Bocas del Toro, zip-lining in Chiriquí, and swimming in Starfish Beach. With all these amazing experiences, taking a canoe ride to a remote island in the rain forest to visit the indigenous Emberá may have been the most surreal. To see a people who still live like they have for hundreds of years is profound. We danced with them, watched them make jewelry, and even ate a meal with our hands cooked by them on palm leaves.

The thing about traveling that I enjoy so much is that it takes me out of my normal routine and reminds me to stay humble. Sometimes we get so caught up in our day-to-day that it begins to feel like our little world is everything. Travel forces you outside the daily routine. In Panama I saw kids in Bocas del Toro who wore dirty clothes, had no shoes, and played kickball with an empty plastic water jug they filled with rags. What struck me about these kids is that they were having the time of their lives! They were so happy, laughing and playing without a care in the world. I thought of how when I played soccer, each season I got a fresh, clean uniform, shiny new cleats, shin guards, and my very own regulation-sized soccer ball to practice with. And while there is absolutely nothing wrong with being able to afford the luxuries of a new uniform and cleats, we take it so much for granted. This is just one example of how exploring different places makes you open your eyes to a much broader reality. The world is bigger than we think; it has so many different cultures, beliefs, values, and customs, and forces you to look beyond yourself. Aside from the adventures and the amazing memories, traveling has also given me a broader perspective about life and made me appreciate what I have just that much more. I'm always dreaming of the next spot we'll visit. I dream of seeing the world, and I dream of meeting you while I do.

Story Time
THE DAY I ALMOST DIED

Here's the downside of having an active mind: sometimes things can get a liiiiiittle out of hand, given that I tend to envision the worst-case scenario unfolding and totally freak out. I know coming down with the flu doesn't sound particularly dramatic or out of the ordinary—everyone gets sick. But let's just put it this way: if anyone is looking for a nail-biting new plotline for *Grey's Anatomy*, look no further: I was a freakin' medical miracle!

We had a flight to LA and needed to be at the airport by 3:00 a.m. Once we got up in the air, I wasn't feeling great—my throat hurt, my nose was stuffy, and as the time ticked by, I was dizzy with chills and burning up with a fever. I chalked it up to having had to get up way too early. But by the time we arrived, I was so, so sick I could barely stand up. I was supposed to have a photo shoot, but my eyes were all bloodshot and my head was pounding.

"That's it," my mom announced. "We're going to urgent

care." We sat in the waiting room and they took about ten years to call me in. Not so urgent, as it turned out!

"So," the doctor said after he had poked and prodded me, "your strep test is negative."

"Then why do I feel so lousy?" I asked.

He scratched his head. "It could be the flu."

It made sense. I had flu-like symptoms. Then I showed him my arms—they were kind of swollen and tingly, and the veins looked very pronounced, like they were popping out.

The doctor's face turned white. "You have to go to the ER—now! You need to be seen by a specialist."

My heart started pounding and my mind raced to a million terrifying scenarios all leading to one conclusion: I had contracted some rare, horrible, incurable, fatal disease (probably on the plane) and now it was too late to save me.

"Oh my god," I told my family as they rushed me out the door. "I saw this happen to a kid once on *Grey's Anatomy* and he died! I'm dying!" Then I burst out crying in complete hysteria. My mom was panicking like she always does in stressful situations, Dad was pretty calm, and Jacob was on his phone, oblivious to the chaos erupting around him. Somehow, we managed to get to the ER of a nearby hospital. But when we walked inside, it was empty, except for one guy staring blankly at the TV on the wall—a total

ghost town with no one there to help me.

"That's it," my mom declared. "We're going somewhere else!" So out we headed again, this time to hospital number two across town with me crumpled up in the back seat of the car, bawling and writing my last will and testament in my head. When we arrived, this ER was packed—I swear, there were about five thousand people waiting to be seen. My mom pushed everyone aside and got me to the front of the line: "My daughter is very sick!" she screamed. "She needs her blood drawn! NOW!"

The lady at reception tried to calm her down: "We'll see her soon but there are a lot of people here waiting. It could take three or four hours."

Three to four hours? How did they know I had three to four hours left? Couldn't they see this was CLEEEEARLY a life-or-death situation? Couldn't they see I was a dead girl walking?

While my mom continued to drive the nurses up the walls, my dad suggested I go back to the car with Jacob to sleep and wait. I passed out from stress and exhaustion, and the next thing I knew, we were pulling up again to urgent care, right back where we started. Apparently, the Martins aren't the most patient people. I looked down at my arms: amazingly, the swelling had gone down and I was sweating—my fever had clearly broken.

The first doctor who had started my entire day from hell saw me again. "Well, I guess we can just take your blood here." Ummmmm, WHAT?? Why didn't you just do that in the first place?????

In the end, it turned out it *was* the flu (not an incurable fatal disease) and he gave me a shot in the butt that hurt like hell. But I was all better in two days and I had a great video about my horrific ordeal to share.

Like I said: life with me is never boring.

Baby Steps

WHAT TO DO
WHEN YOU HAVE NOTHING TO DO?

We all have some days when we need to chill out and relax. That's when I . . .

Binge-watch Netflix. I usually do this with my friends and family so we can talk about it after. I've recently been watching the series *The End of the F***ing World*, and my parents and I have had some really deep talks about stuff that goes on between the characters. I'll also watch movies and I have a ton of favorites that I've seen over and over again. Thrillers are my favorite genre: they mess with your mind and have twists and puzzles to solve. A few I love are *Primal Fear* (because it's soooo smart and Ed Norton is the best most wonderful actor in the universe), *Fight Club* (Ed Norton again! Would ya look at that!! He and Leonardo DiCaprio are my favorite actors), *Silence of the*

Lambs, *Seven*, *Gone Baby Gone*, and *The Usual Suspects*. I also adore a great love story. Some of my favorites are *Titanic* (I could watch that over and over, and of course, it's got Leonardo), *The Notebook* (basically any Nicholas Sparks movie reduces me to a puddle of tears), and *Love, Rosie*. That one is a cute story about a boy and girl who are best friends who actually love each other and SHOULD be together but are afraid they'll mess up their friendship if they go for it and SAY IT. Hmmmm, kinda sounds like a crush I'm familiar with . . .

Check out videos on YouTube and other social media. Weston Koury cracks me up; he is such an out-of-the-box thinker and has a twisted sense of humor. I also love Miranda Sings; she is my all-time favorite YouTuber. For the record, my mom is obsessed with her and sometimes slips into the Miranda voice without even realizing she's doing it. I also looooove Orion Carloto. She's just very genuine and I relate to her story times so much. I watch Best Vines compilations as well as singers and performers, like Bruno Mars, Kehlani, SZA, Britney Spears, and Prince. I like to see the way they create a great experience for their audience from the stage with their music and I aspire to bring that to my audience someday. I could also spend an entire day checking Twitter and following my friends on

Snapchat, Instagram, and musical.ly. I just love people's creativity and I always feel so inspired.

Call a friend to catch up. We all have different friends that fulfill different needs. Not any one person checks off all the boxes and that's okay. I have different conversations with different friends under different circumstances. With some friends, I can get really deep and talk about things that are very meaningful, like religion and political beliefs. With other friends, I have lighter conversations about things like clothes, makeup, or what's going on with Kylie and Khloe. Sometimes, I seek out a friend who can give me a hug through the phone if I'm going through a tough time. Other times, I am content to have a lighthearted conversation that allows me to be silly.

Play some board games. We love our family game nights! At least once a week we turn off all electronics after dinner, pull out some games, put on some music, and start playing. It's also become a tradition to host family and friends game night where we invite friends over, order some pizza, and make a day of it. Some of our favorites are backgammon, Clue, Pictionary, Yahtzee, Risk, Balderdash, and Monopoly, but we are always open to something new. On our last family trip to South Carolina, my cousin Keira introduced us to a game called Exploding Kittens. Sounds strange, I know, but we played nonstop! We also enjoy video games; we have a Nintendo Switch and just got an Xbox. We are currently obsessed with *Fortnite*—Jacob and I could play that for hours. It's the video game equivalent of *The Hunger Games*. Games are just such an amazing way to disconnect from the world and spend fun time laughing with people you love.

Get in the kitchen and cook. I'm not gonna lie, I'm not a good cook. The extent of my skills is making mac 'n' cheese in the microwave, but thankfully my mom is! There is nothing that replaces some bonding time with Mom in the kitchen. I may not be a chef, but I can follow directions and help, or at least just watch!

RECIPE: SHARON'S HOMEMADE SPAGHETTI AND MEAT SAUCE

Ingredients

¼ cup extra virgin olive oil

1 large onion, coarsely chopped

3 garlic cloves, peeled and coarsely chopped

1 celery stalk, coarsely chopped

1 carrot, coarsely chopped

1 pound ground beef

½ pound ground lamb
1 28-ounce can crushed tomatoes
¼ cup parsley, chopped
8 basil leaves, chopped
1 large bay leaf
1 tablespoon sage, chopped
Salt and pepper
Parmesan cheese

In a large pot over medium-high heat, heat the olive oil. Add the onion and garlic, and sauté until the onions become translucent. Add the chopped celery and carrots and sauté for 4–6 minutes, stirring occasionally. Raise heat to high and add the ground beef and lamb. Sauté the meat for about 10 minutes, stirring frequently and breaking up any large clumps. When meat is cooked through (no longer pink), add the can of crushed tomatoes and all chopped fresh herbs: parsley, basil, and sage. Add the bay leaf. Stir ingredients together for a few minutes, then reduce heat to low, cover pot, and let sauce simmer for about an hour. Remove bay leaf and discard. Season with salt and pepper. Serve over spaghetti and top with lots of Parmesan cheese.

#askAriel

I have NOTHING to do this summer. I'm sixteen, and I don't want to work in Pizza Hut like my mom suggests. What would you do if you were me?

Journal! Start writing down your dreams, your thoughts, your fears. Pretend you're writing a love letter to your crush! Also, try totally different things, things you might be a little afraid of. Make that YouTube channel you've always wanted and start posting. Reach out to someone at school you've always thought was kind of cool but were afraid to talk to. Listen to music that's from a new genre or artist. Dream up something you've always wanted to be or do and go for it! As for working, I'm all for it—it's a great way to make money so you can buy yourself a great back-to-school wardrobe. If Pizza Hut doesn't appeal, find something that does: work with kids at a pool, animals at a vet's office, or ask your favorite store if they need some extra hands (maybe they'll also give you a discount!). Instead of looking at the summer as nothing to do, look at it as an amazing opportunity to launch a whole new you. Think of it as a three-month pass to explore things that make you happy and excited.

Okay, so I got my learner's permit but I'm freaked out to actually drive. How do I get over my road phobia?
I totally get it! I'm still afraid to drive, and I blame my mom for that—she freaks out and starts screaming, "Watch out! Look where you're going!" when we're driving anywhere, even just down the block in our neighborhood. But you gotta learn, right? So, find someone who is totally calm (not my mom) and a good driver and get them to take you to an empty parking lot (or somewhere there are no cars or people at all) and practice, practice, practice. Keep at it till you get comfortable behind the wheel, and pretty soon you'll be on the road without a worry.

My friends are picking on me because I refuse to smoke and vape with them. What should I do?
You do you! It's really hard to resist pressure from your friends, and I am so proud of you for knowing that it's

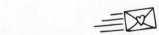

wrong for you to smoke and vape and having the courage to say no. Tell them that you're just not into it and that you want them to respect your decision. If they're true friends, they'll respect you and stop giving you pressure. If not, find some new friends who can figure out better things to do with their time!

Free-falling

My first DigiFest was in September 2017 in Texas, and it was the first time I had to go onstage in front of a huge, live audience of social-media-obsessed fans. I went on right after Nash Grier, who was really big—I mean, the guy had millions of subscribers on YouTube while I was just breaking into all of this. I had to follow that act and I was terrified. I was convinced the girls in the audience wouldn't like me. They were there to see cute YouTube boys and wouldn't be happy one bit when I came out onstage. I worried there would be boos, rotten tomatoes thrown at me, a huge hook pulling me back behind the curtains—normal stuff. But

I decided I had to do it; I had to take the chance. After all, my dream was on the line and I couldn't chicken out simply because I wasn't sure how people would react. I had to focus on the here and now. I would never know if I could do it unless I actually *did* it—funny how that works. And if someone was going to boo me off, then I had to block it out and just do me. One of my favorite quotes is "We always regret the decisions that we did not make . . ." So I decided I *had* to do this. I had to take that leap.

Thankfully, things worked out for me—I mustered up as much confidence as I could, put a big smile on my face, grabbed a mic, went out on the stage, and greeted everyone with, "Hi, guys! Are you all having a good time?" They cheered wildly and clapped (nobody threw any tomatoes!) and I finally relaxed a bit. Focusing my attention on the crowd and how they were feeling took the pressure off myself. After Arii and I introduced ourselves, we lip-synched and danced to our favorite Nicki Minaj song and played an interactive lip-synch battle with the audience and 5Quad. The audience loved us!

The tour helped grow my following tremendously and gave me a lot of confidence. It also made me realize I wanted to be a go-getter, the kind of person who doesn't let insecurity hold her back. I've come to appreciate that there are a lot of great reasons why you should go for it. First off, it proves to yourself and the rest of the world that you're brave. Risk is scary; it's hurling yourself into the unknown and facing uncertainty. You're doing something that might have a bad outcome. But then again: maybe it won't! The point is you don't know and you can't know . . . until you do it. Taking a risk makes you feel powerful, like nothing and nobody can stand in your way. It proves that you've got guts, and guts equal glory. It shows that you're open to new experiences and ideas and finding out new things about yourself. Every time I take a risk, I learn something knew about myself. Most of the time, it's that I'm bolder, braver, and more creative than I ever thought.

The scariest thing I have probably ever done in my entire life is deciding to launch a recording career. Ever since I was little, music has been one of the biggest parts of my life. My dad plays piano and sings every single day, and I've been taking piano and singing lessons for a long time. It's always been a way for me to express myself, but putting out your own music—that's a lot different than singing into your hairbrush in your bedroom. I was petrified (and still am, just a little) that people wouldn't like my sound or think I could legit sing after being known as a muser. Every time a new song or video comes out, I'm a nervous wreck, a combination of super excited and super paranoid. I want my fans to love what I've made because I've poured my heart and soul into it. Even though I make very personal videos sharing all aspects of my life all the time, singing takes me to a very vulnerable place. But I knew I had to push past my doubts and insecurities and confront my fears head on. Sometimes the thing that scares you the most turns out to be the thing that helps you grow the most. It's about discovering things about yourself you never knew. You're opening yourself up to rejection and baring your soul—that's scary stuff. I used to think that if you felt vulnerable, it meant you weren't strong. Now I think it's just the opposite: it takes a tremendous amount of courage to let people see the real you and to put everything out there, even the things you're not comfortable and confident showing. And when you do this, when you allow people in, you form a really deep connection.

I had some specific rules for how I was going to go about making my music: I was really determined that my songs would sound like me and come from my life and experiences so my audience could relate. They had to be an extension of my authentic self, not a fake version of me. "Perf" is about the exciting, bubbly feeling you have when you're totally crushing on someone at the beginning of a relationship. But it's also about having enough self-respect to know who you are, and being confident about what you want and what you expect in a relationship. The writing sessions for me were the hardest and most nerve-racking, even more than the recording. I'm used to curling up on my bed with a journal and writing a song, not locked in a room with four other people, sitting in a circle and talking about my feelings. It was weird—a little like therapy!—and definitely took some getting used to. My opinion is usually the only one that counts when it comes to what I put out there—no one tells me what YouTube videos to make or how to make them. But all of a sudden, there were other people who got to have a say because there's a record label involved and the music business is serious business. Most of the time I got my way—I have a really strong vision (and I'm sorta stubborn), especially when it comes to the videos. But what people might not know or understand about the production process on an album is how collaborative it is. That's why it's so important to surround yourself with people you trust and to listen to their advice. I had no idea going into this what I was doing; I have gotten so much better at it because I had great, smart, experienced people to guide me and I was open to learning from them.

The first song I ever recorded was called "Bad Pics." We recorded it at my friend Daniel's home studio, and that made it more comfortable for me. It was a familiar place and I'd met the engineer before through Daniel. The writer also came in and she helped me connect to the words. It took twelve hours to lay down the vocals! For my second session, recording "Aww," it was just me, my mom, and the engineer. This time, there were even fewer nerves; I knew what to expect and I was able to get out of my head and just enjoy it. About six or seven months went by before we actually released my debut single, "Aww." I had it in my hands; I could listen to it and love it, but I couldn't share it or let my fans know about it—we were waiting for the perfect timing. Which meant that the day it finally came out, it felt a little weird that suddenly everyone could listen to it. It had been only mine for so long, and now I was setting it free into the universe. I didn't want to set any expectations for myself; I didn't think, "I won't be happy unless it hits the Top 100 on iTunes." All I wanted was for people to like it and to relate to it. Then my manager called and said, "Ariel, you're number forty-five on the iTunes pop chart." WHAAAT?!!? Are you kidding me????? That's insane! It now has six million streams on Spotify, too, and over forty million views on YouTube.

Shooting music videos is also a really amazing experience for me. I'm so used to making my YouTube videos or musical.lys and 99 percent of the time, it's me alone with my camera or iPhone. But shooting a music video professionally means working with a whole crew. There are literally dozens of people running around, trying to get things done. There's the camera crew, the lighting crew, directors and assistant directors, hair and makeup, even caterers. And of course, there's the cast. Working on the "Aww" video was so much fun because I got to have a bunch of my really good friends be with me in it. It meant so much to have support from friends like Daniel, Max & Harvey, Zach, Patrick, Arii, Matthew, Charles, Bryce, and Brennen. We laughed, threw balls at each other, chased puppies, and played with kids to make the video. Our goal was to have people watch the video and go, "Aww," to themselves (by the reaction it got, I feel like mission accomplished!). One of the funniest things, though, was the last shot of the day. We got my friend Matthew Taylor to do his makeup (which he's amazing at) and look like a porcelain doll. We then poured paint on him and shot it in super slow-motion while he stared motionless at the camera. When you look at the video, it's an amazing effect. However, there was a big problem we realized afterward: there were no towels or a shower at the studio! Poor Matthew had to literally rinse gallons of paint off his body under a sink and dry off with paper towels!

Shooting "Perf" was also a ton of fun but in a very different way. We thought it would be neat to play on the idea that in fact, nobody really is perfect. So I played a character who kept getting broken up with by really

Me as a one-year-old, eating my favorite food and making a big mess.

Look, Mom! I have two teeth now; I'm growing up.

Clowning around! My grandmother (Safta) made my costume for the Jewish holiday Purim—it was a replica of what she'd made my mom when she was my age.

Baby Jacob is on his way! I couldn't wait to meet my new brother.

We found this cow outside a restaurant in Miami, so of course we had to climb it! With Jacob and our cousins Nick, Katia, and Mateo.

OMG! My brother's first kiss and I was there to witness it. What a stud!

Believe it or not, I was actually pretty good at soccer. My dad was the best coach!

Our family on a beautiful hot-air balloon ride in Park City, Utah. We crash-landed in a residential neighborhood! Only us!

My dancing days. I was so flexible.

(from left to right) Grandpa Bernie, Grandma (Safta) Ayala, Jacob, Uncle Dan, Uncle Ronen, me, Mom, Aunt Sara, and Aunt Anat at the Western Wall in Jerusalem, Israel.

Practicing for my third piano recital. Who knew I'd be writing my own songs all these years later?

Dressed up as candy corn for my elementary school Halloween party.

My bat mitzvah day, right before the service. You can't tell, but I was sooooo nervous!

A family photo on my first trip to Panama with my ginormous Panamanian family! I love each and every one of them.

In Austin, Texas, all ready for a friend's bat mitzvah.

My first ever live show in LA. I was beyond excited!

Behind the scenes of my second music video, "Perf," with my "boyfriend," Derek (Morgan) Perfman.

On the red carpet at the Latin Billboard Music Awards. I saw Jennifer Lopez! What a goddess!

A quick mirror selfie before a photo shoot at my uncle Dan's house (he cleaned his bathroom for me and everything!).

Making a quick musical.ly at a photo shoot in my favorite teddy bear sweater.

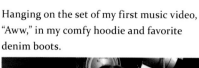

Hanging on the set of my first music video, "Aww," in my comfy hoodie and favorite denim boots.

On the set of my "Perf" music video.

On a trip to NYC. Mom and I had to do a quick run to buy coats—we underestimated how freezing we would be!

One of my favorite merch items. That's me on the T-shirt stuffing my face.
Who wants cake??

In the dressing room getting dolled up for
the cover shoot for this book!

A snapshot from my "Aww" music video.

cute boys. To take matters into my own hands, I ordered a mannequin and made him my "Perf" boyfriend! At first, it was kind of weird having this mannequin on the set just kind of sitting there. So to make it less creepy, I decided to have fun with him and make it more "natural." I named him Derek after my TV crush, Derek Morgan from *Criminal Minds*. Pretty soon, everyone on the set was calling him Derek. The director would yell, "Hey, Derek, get on set! You're late for your shot!" I even saw my dad talking to him and telling him that he better treat me right! We had a blast and it made the day go by so much better. Until of course, I had to cram him in a car. For one of the scenes, I had to pretend to rush Derek into the back seat and speed away from a group of girls who were chasing us. The problem was that Derek was actually waaay taller and heavier than me. So imagine, little Ariel lugging this huge mannequin into a tiny car. Then, when I finally got him there, he wouldn't fit in the back seat! I nearly broke him into five pieces just to grab that shot. By the end, I was exhausted but we were all laughing like crazy. Making videos alone for YouTube or musical.ly is fun, but there's really nothing quite like working with a team of people. I encourage you to step out of your comfort zone and find a few friends to work together with. You'll have more fun and you'll learn new things about yourself and each other.

So after all that hard work, has everybody had nice things to say about my foray into music? Well, ya know haters gonna hate. But there's also been a ton of love, an outpouring of support and enthusiasm that's made me even more determined to keep going in this direction. You know what honestly blows my mind? There are people making musical.lys of my songs! They're doing the hand motions and facial gestures and it's my voice they're lip-synching to! It's so weird and so amazing at the same time—and definitely full circle for me. If you'd ever told me this would be my life, I would have told you that you were nuts!

Lights, Camera, Me

So I was binge-watching the YouTube series *Chicken Girls*, and was obsessed with how the first season was going to end. I tweeted how much I loved the quirky teenage comedy and before I knew it, my friend Hayden, who plays one of the main characters, reached out and asked if I'd want to do a guest spot on the show! It was a lot of fun, and I guess the people who created the show liked what I did, because all of a sudden, we were talking about creating a show around *me*. Initially, I was in shock: "Really? No way! Are you serious? For real?" When they convinced me they meant it, the ideas started flowing, and they wanted me to be a part of the brainstorming process. At first, they thought it would be a show about a girl boss who has her own nail polish company. But music is so much on my brain, I suggested the girl boss create her own record label. *Baby Doll Records* was born! I got to help develop the story, and select the cast. The producers wanted my feedback and approval for everything, and pretty soon they agreed that I was an executive producer for the show! I have to say, it all happened very quickly. We shot seven episodes in what felt like a split second (it was really about three weeks of

12–14-hour days). And my real mom got to play my mom (in case you didn't know, she used to do theater and is an amazing actress), my brother Jacob got to play my little bro, and my BFF Matthew played my BFF in the show. Sorry Dad, your acting isn't quite up to snuff!

My character's name is Dru, and she's different from me in a lot of ways, but also similar in her ambition and drive. I love her fashion sense and might borrow her style by wearing bandannas! In the show, Dru dreams of being a record producer, but her parents don't support her. I can't imagine what that's like (that's why they call it acting) because my own parents have always been so supportive of me. But Dru figures it out; she may have to go behind their backs sometimes and pull some crazy stunts, but it's all in the name of achieving her goals, and it makes the series pretty hysterically funny. In a way, Dru really embodies what it means to "dream out loud" because she knows what she wants and goes after it.

The process of shooting a series was great but also intense. I put a lot of pressure on myself. My mom would be like, "You did amazing in that scene!" and I would be stressed and nitpicking my performance. We also had to shoot a lot in a limited amount of time. I'm someone who likes to really think about a scene and talk it over with the director, but there were days where I would have to quickly memorize my script and jump into hair and makeup and just do it.

Here's the craziest thing: it made me want to get involved in acting and producing even more. Since I was a little kid, I'd always liked acting. I'd play dress-up and do "plays" for my parents all the time. And I got my first taste of professional acting when I guest-starred in the holiday episode of Disney's *Bizaardvark*. I had such fun that I knew I'd want to do even more acting. But getting to be involved in every part of the process, from developing the story to finding the actors to working with the director made me realize how much I love everything about filmmaking. Anyone who knows me already knows I'm obsessed with movies and great shows. But getting to make my own entire series sparked something inside me. You know that feeling when you get giddy butterflies in your stomach? When you can't help smiling because something makes you so incredibly happy and fulfilled? That's how I felt, so I know I am on to something. I have a passion that I now want to pursue even more strongly. One day, I'd like to write, direct, produce, and star in my own movie. It goes to show that when an opportunity comes along, even if it's something you weren't sure was your "thing," it's worth trying. You never know what will come of it, what will light that fire. So Hollywood, here I come!

Story Time

THE RIDE OF MY LIFE

I have been on dozens of roller coasters and all kinds of thrill rides. I was never scared to go on any of them, not even the crazy upside-down, backward, loop-de-loop ones. Then I found myself facing Dr. Doom's Fearfall at Universal's Islands of Adventure. If you haven't experienced it, allow me to explain: they climb you up, up, up to the top of some insanely high tower then drop you down, down, down at what feels like a million miles per hour. Of course, my friends wanted to go on it the minute we set foot in the theme park, and of course, I was terrified.

"It's okay—you guys go on without me," I said, waving them on. I figured I'd just sit on a bench, eat my ice cream pop, and no one would care. But they were insistent I stop being a wimp and try it. I felt a strangely familiar feeling of panic setting in. Then I remembered why: when I was ten, I went on one of these stupid free-fall rides and I thought I was going to die.

"I'm gonna cry my eyes out. I'm gonna hate it," I told my best friends. It was this whole trauma situation with me freaking out, and them trying to calm me down and convince me to do it.

"Come on," they pleaded with me. "It'll be so much fun!"

I looked up at the ride. That thing was freakin' high! Like, thirteen stories high. I knew it was also pitch dark and spooky inside, and the fact that they had a warning posted for pregnant women or people with high blood pressure or back injuries was not helping my nerves. But since I was none of the above, I decided it was time to suck it up.

"Fine," I finally gave in. "I'll do it. I'll hate it, but I'll do it." I saw how excited my friends were and what a great time they were having, and I didn't want to be the Debbie Downer in the group.

Here's the worst part: you have to wait on this mile-long line, even with fast passes, to actually get on the ride. This gave me plenty of time to talk myself out of it. I contemplated all the possible outcomes of what would happen as soon as they strapped me in: I'd cry, scream, faint, throw up, beg them to stop and let me off, pee myself, cause a huge scene and be tossed out of the park by security.

Then, suddenly, we were at the front of the line and

it was my turn. I literally felt my heart free-fall into my stomach, and the tears welled up in my eyes.

"You okay?" my friend asked me.

Do I look okay? Do I look like I am *happy* about this situation? I think NOT!!!

As we entered, I tried to talk myself off the ledge: Ariel, it will all be over in a few seconds. You can do this. There are little kids going on this thing and they're not freaking out like you are. Man up! But the creepy Dr. Doom music was definitely getting to me. The ride operator strapped us into the seats. I kept checking to make sure that the shoulder harness was secured because I was SURE that it was going to open up and that I'd go flying through the park and go SPLAT on the pavement of the park. My friends were laughing and yelling. Me, I was just trying not to pee myself. Then we slowly lifted just a bit off the ground. My feet lifted off the ground and I thought, "Welp, this is it Ariel. It's been nice knowin' ya." Then, just like that, it shot us straight up in the air like a rocket. I felt adrenaline rushing through me, and suddenly, I could see all of Orlando from what felt like a mile up in the air. We paused there for a second before plunging straight down at a hurtling speed. A few more ups and downs. Then it was over. Just like that. I lived, and I LOVED it. I wanted to go on again.

My friends got to say, "Told ya so," and I got over my fear of free-fall rides. In fact, they're now my favorites because there is nothing quite like the adrenaline rush of that drop. I went on this ride thinking I was going to die, but I came off it feeling incredibly alive, and most important, proud of myself. I conquered Dr. Doom and my fear of falling. Ready for skydiving. Yay, me!

6 THINGS THAT FREAK ME OUT

Most people harbor irrational fears—and I'm no exception . . .

1. Lizards. They live in my front yard and they pop out of nowhere with their beady little eyes. If I see one, I run in the other direction—usually screaming.

2. Snakes coming out of my sink or toilet. It's not likely that this will actually ever happen, but I've heard of it happening to other people, so it's always something that I think about whenever I'm around indoor plumbing and it totally creeps me out.

3. Tornados. I remember having a dream when I was little of getting sucked up by a tornado and it scarred me for life. Clearly, I am never ever going to watch the movie "Twister". . . .

4. Shots or getting blood drawn. I completely lose it when they come at me with that needle and I know it's going to hurt. I never believe them when they say, "You'll feel just a pinch." It's not a pinch—it's pain! My mom has to hold my hand and I have to cover my eyes and lie down—it's a very dramaful event.

5. Failure. I admit it, I do worry sometimes about all of this just going away. What if I wake up tomorrow and nobody likes me anymore? What if no one knows or cares who I am or what I have to say? What if I lose every single one of my fans? It's why I push myself to work really, really hard because I don't want this to end. I want to always be doing what I love and doing it the very best I can.

6. Melted cheese. Yeah, really!!!

Baby Steps

HOW TO KICK FEAR TO THE CURB

Okay, time to get a grip. If I can do it, you can do it.

Come clean. Admit what you're afraid of—don't try to keep it all pent up inside. Accept the anxiety you're feeling and tell someone (a friend, a parent, a teacher) if you think it's holding you back. Just saying the words can be liberating. Or write down your fears in your journal so you can get them out of your head and prove them wrong.

Picture the fear playing out in your head. Kind of like watching a movie, see yourself confronting your worst nightmare. I know, not fun. But trust me when I tell you there's a method to this madness! See the thing that's scaring you, then visualize a safe and secure outcome: You're okay! You survived! No giant lizard ate you for lunch—wait, that's my nightmare, not yours. This way, you'll feel prepared to handle the worst scenario, which FYI, will probably never happen.

If your fear is big, break it down into smaller pieces. Let's say you're petrified of speaking in public and you have to give a speech in front of the entire tenth grade. Start slow: practice speaking in front of your mom, then a few close friends, then maybe your homeroom class. With each tiny task you accomplish, your confidence will grow.

Breathe. I know that sounds pretty obvious, but when faced with anxiety, sometimes we forget. Focus on taking a deep breath in, holding it for a few seconds, and then letting the air out slowly. This technique actually slows your racing heart and calms you down. You could even close your eyes and chant "om" if it makes you happy.

Distract yourself. Whenever I'm feeling afraid, I will do anything to take my mind off it. Jump on your phone and scroll through your Instagram feed, even if you don't really feel like it—your brain has a hard time doing two things at once, so if it's otherwise occupied, it won't be freaking out. I have game apps and lots of music on my phone expressly for this reason.

Tell someone. Talk out your fears—sometimes just saying them out loud and getting things off your chest makes a situation less scary. I will vent to my mom or my friends if I need to soothe my nerves. Even if I don't get sympathy, I'll get, "Ariel, that's ridiculous! That's not gonna happen!" and it snaps me out of the fear spiral. When you verbalize what you're afraid of, suddenly you're taking it off you; you're letting someone else help you shoulder it. And let's not underestimate the value of a hug (which usually comes after I've poured my heart out and I'm a hysterical mess). I don't know about you, but when I'm scared, I like to hug it out.

Talk to a professional. If all else fails and you feel consumed by your fear, it may be time to enlist the help of a therapist, and there is no shame in that. When anxiety takes over and is affecting the quality of your life, that's a sign that you need a little extra help from a professional. You wouldn't hesitate to call your doctor if you had a sore throat, right?

#askariel

For my sixteenth birthday I asked my parents to let me go skydiving. I got a big "No way!" Shouldn't it be my decision?

I feel you! I've wanted to skydive since I was, like, twelve but my parents won't let me, either. They always say that until I'm eighteen, they are completely responsible for me and for my safety, so no parachuting out of an airplane juuuust yet. I've decided to respect their decision and wait it out a few more years and would suggest you do the same. Try indoor skydiving (it's a lot less dangerous) and go on roller coasters instead. Then, when you're officially an adult, you can jump out of planes to your heart's content. I don't think your parents will be any less nervous about it, but at that point (hopefully) they will be okay with you making your own choices.

I'm feeling really stressed out lately—tests, college applications, school drama. What do you do to de-stress?

I stress whenever I get too in my head. I think the best thing you can do is find ways to get out of your head and your feelings. Put your stress away for an hour or two—you won't miss it. I like to do creative things like journal, sit at my piano and play, or doodle. I also dance and sing or go outside and just chill. Look at the clouds and stars! The key is to distract yourself so you're not thinking about all the drama and that mile-long to-do list. Just know you're not alone—as teenagers, we face an awful lot of stress because we're growing up and figuring out our futures and who we want to be. My parents always remind me that they also went through this and so did their parents and their parents before them; everyone does. You'll get through it, I promise!

I have this irrational fear of escalators! When I was three, I fell on one and needed stitches in my chin. I always think it will happen again, so I avoid them at movie theaters and malls. I'm so embarrassed for my friends to see me freaking out and taking the stairs if we go shopping!

Okay, you were three. Let's just agree that you are way more coordinated today than you were as a toddler. Kids take lots of falls; I was always tripping over my own two feet and skinning my knees. Let's not blame the escalator; it might have had little to do with it. My advice to you is practice. Ask your mom or dad to take you to the mall and try getting on and off the escalator with them. Then do it a couple of times on your own. If you see you can do it without incident, I'm sure the fear will gradually go away. Just don't beat yourself up for feeling afraid. We all have weird stuff that scares us. At least you don't think a python is living in your toilet bowl like I do!

YELLOW is a sunshiny color. It boosts my confidence and reminds me to be happy. It's also the color of friendship—people who are true and loyal to you.

You do you

I was out one night with a bunch of friends and this boy, for some reason, decided to throw some shade on my shoes. He's a good kid and we're still friends; I think he was mainly trying to be funny, and it just turned out to be at my expense. I had just been on a photo shoot and had fallen in love with these high-top Pumas, so I'd been psyched to wear them out that night. We were eating dinner, and he literally grabbed my foot from under the table and pulled it out to show everyone.

"Oh my god, look at these shoes she's wearing. They're boxing shoes!" Everyone at the table burst out laughing and suddenly the discussion became all about my questionable taste in footwear.

I felt my cheeks flush and I found myself getting defensive: "I think they're cute! I love them." No one was really hearing me; they were too busy cracking up and shoe-shaming me. So Arii (love that girl!) pipes up, "What are you guys talking about? They *are* cute. Shut up!" And they did. And the conversation moved on.

But it dawned on me: when did people get so judgy? What's wrong with simply wearing something that makes you feel good about yourself? What gives anyone the right to tell me how to dress, act, live? Are you gonna order my food for me, too?

If you haven't noticed, I do my own thing. I am not someone who particularly cares about fitting in; frankly, I'd rather stand out. I like my nails long, my hoops big, and my makeup glam. I am who I am! But not everyone feels that way about themselves; I think teenagers in particular worry about belonging, and they think they have to look a certain way or do certain things for their peers to accept them. When I was in high school, I saw a lot of kids compromising who they were just to seem cool. That negative peer pressure can lead to drinking, drugs, and other stuff you do not want to get involved in. What's the point? What's the goal? To be a mindless clone? The last thing I want is for someone to squash my creativity and individuality. If you don't want me in your club, so be it. I don't want to be a part of any group that doesn't sing each other's praises. My shoe choice might not be yours. Or maybe you wouldn't pick my hair color or the jeans I'm wearing. That's okay; we don't need to be twinning. I don't think I've ever dressed *exactly* like my friends; my clothes have always had a bit of my personal Ariel-ness to them. And honestly, I'm okay with that and you should be, too. I find that people who bring others down usually have really low self-esteem. They don't think they're good enough, so they try to be someone they're not, both in behavior and appearance.

Personally, I believe in respect over everything else. You respect me, I'll respect you, and that includes my clothes, my feelings, my beliefs, my politics, my opinions—even if they differ from yours. You don't have to agree with me or even like what I wear or do, but you need to *respect* it. And in case you haven't already figured this one out, pretending to be someone you're not is exhausting, exasperating, and depressing! You always feel like you're on and you can't just relax and be yourself. You will never—I repeat, *never*—be pleased with yourself if all you do is spend your time trying to please everyone else. At some point, you have to make the choice to march to your own drum. The people who appreciate your brand of specialness are the ones you want in your life. The ones who try to force you to conform—they don't deserve you. Did you know that no two snowflakes are alike? Be a snowflake—and anyone who doesn't like it can chill.

HATERS GONNA HATE

While most of the comments I receive on social media are loving and supportive (my fan-mily is the best), I've had my share of downright mean and evil ones. For no reason! People have made hateful comments about me without knowing me, which is really dumb and a little desperate, if you ask me. I've had to develop a pretty thick skin and either ignore or delete them. A few times I posted some videos of me reacting just to prove that I don't care or let them bother me. In one, Arii and I were cracking up at all the hate we get, stuff like, "Your facial expressions look like a cross between a witch and a Chihuahua" and "You're so ugly it makes me want to throw up in my mouth." I mean, how does a person even respond to that? But in the beginning, when I was just fourteen and starting out, it was kind of a *rude* awakening. I put up a musical.ly or a video I was proud of, and suddenly the hate started coming at me. How bad was it?

"Eww."

"You suck."

"Your hair is hideous."

"What is your real talent? Nada."

"I hate you."

"I don't know who told you your eyes were pretty because they look like boogers."

Need I go on? Is that the best you people got? Boogerlicious eyes? I can laugh at it now, but my mom spent the first several weeks of my social media debut reading and deleting every single nasty remark. She was really freaked out by it. The first few times it happened, the hate literally hurt my heart. I was so proud of what I was doing and this felt like someone just slapped me in the face. I felt like it was eating me up inside. So I made a video reacting to the hate comments and I momentarily felt better. I made fun of all those ugly remarks and threw back a few insults of my own. But then I questioned: What's the point? What am I accomplishing? What do I get out of being mean to someone, even if they were mean to me in the first place? Nothing. So I made another video. This one talked about the fact that you can't control the nasty things people say about you, but you can control how you react to them. You can choose to remain positive and choose love over hate. When I watch it now, I realize I was feeling all these emotions while I made it and trying to stay strong and be a role model for kids who were being bullied. As the day went on, I got all these comments from people about how much they really connected to that video and how watching it helped them. It got nearly a million views. I commented back, and we started sharing our stories and building each other up. That's when I realized this was exactly what I needed to do: band my fans together so we could wipe out hate with a hashtag!

So that's how it all started: people posting kind, compassionate words, cute pics, fan art, and fun quotables and tagging them #ArielMovement. There are more than 30,000 of these posts now on Instagram alone and I love, love, love them—things like "You are allowed to be both a masterpiece and a work in progress at the same time" or "1 year = 365 opportunities." I post, you post, we all post. The goal is to share positivity and spread it so that love eclipses the hate. We have each other; we can rise above it. You've got my back and I've got yours.

Eventually, I figured out I couldn't let it get to me. It was clearly about them, not me. You can't give it any energy.

Why do people do it? To get attention. To feel like they're more important than someone who has all these followers. To kill time because they're bored and have nothing better to do. In the moment, they think that making you feel bad is going to make them feel better, and you happen to be the one they came across on their Instagram feed that day. It's not you; it's them. And once you realize that, and separate yourself from the situation, no one can hurt you anymore.

If a genie granted me three wishes, I would probably use them all up on getting people to stop bullying. It makes me both angry and sad, and I worry because so many kids are dealing with this on a daily basis and suffering in silence. They feel attacked and alone; some will hurt themselves or even take their own lives to make the pain stop. When will it end? Why do we live in a world where bullying is not only tolerated but accepted? Why do we look the other way when we see hate posted? In my opinion, every school should have a no-tolerance policy as well as anti-bullying educational programs in place so kids are taught compassion, empathy, and respect. Parents should teach it at home as well. It is not okay to call someone ugly or stupid or make fun of their looks on social media. Words are weapons as much as guns and knives, and they can do just as much damage.

HANDLING HATERS

No matter what you do or how well you do it, there will always be someone who loves to rain on your parade for no reason. Whenever you find yourself around these types of toxic people . . .

Don't take the bait. This is what they live for. DO NOT ENGAGE. Way back in the beginning I used to respond to obnoxious comments on my social media because there was a part of me that believed they would change their ways, see the light, maybe even apologize. But inevitably it just fueled them and I'd find myself in the midst of a verbal battle that I didn't sign up for. Bottom line: be an example of positivity by lifting others up and ignoring the haters. Remember, people who make hateful comments are just trying to get a reaction out of you and if they don't get what they want they will eventually go away. Don't let them push your buttons; shut the elevator door in their face!

Try not to take it personally. These people are really unhappy in their own lives and are lashing out at you because they're frustrated, jealous, freaking out over how great you are (and how great they're not). They think bringing you down will raise them up. News flash: it ain't gonna work!

If the hating is happening online, delete it. If it's happening in person and you can't ignore it or feel bullied, talk to someone (your parent, teacher, coach, adviser) who can help you. There are also lots of great anti-bullying organizations out there that can help you handle it.

See a hater as a motivator. Instead of getting upset, realize that if you're pissing them off or making them feel threatened, you must be doing something really right!

Laugh it off. A good sense of humor can get you over any obnoxious comment. Really? Is that the best you got for me?

Be a role model for positivity. Post only kind comments and respect everyone who is using social media in a positive way to express themselves. I think if we all just made it our mission to practice kindness, hating would eventually have no place in social media or the world in general.

Story Time
NAME-CALLING

When I first started getting active on social media, it got quite a reaction in my new high school. I had just started at the school in the ninth grade, and a lot of kids were confused by what I was doing and, frankly, a little envious of all the attention it was getting. I remember I was walking down the hall one day, and this boy I didn't know suddenly shouted at me, "Hey, you're the musical.ly girl! You're famous!"

At first, I thought he was trying to be complimentary or was actually a fan. Then I realized he was laughing and pointing when he said it; he was totally making fun of me. Kids stopped and stared and whispered. It was a totally sucky feeling.

What was worse was he did it *all* the time—basically any time he caught sight of me. "Hey! Famous! Ha-ha!"

I rolled my eyes the first few times; then I decided enough was enough.

I confronted him: "Oh my god, what are you doing? Stop!"

Now he knew I was pissed off. He knew he was getting to me. That only made him want to do it more: "Whoa, look who it is. It's her! From musical.ly!"

The next time it happened, I didn't try to silence him. I ignored the laughter and taunts and kept right on walking past him. I refused to give him the time of day. And eventually, he stopped, probably because he wasn't getting a reaction out of me and the joke was getting old. But I will never forget that feeling of being mocked for being myself. I think if it happened to me today, I would react differently. I would probably take a bow or reply, "Yes, thank you, I am!" But back then, I didn't have that confidence yet. I had to get to the place where I am today, where I'm really proud to be Ariel. And I know I'm a lot more than just my social media, thank you very much—and I'm going to continue to add more to my resume. So that guy better study up if he wants to try to label me again. No one puts this baby in the corner!

Baby Steps

GO YOUR OWN WAY

If everybody did the same thing, we'd be zombie clones. Do what makes you *you*. Sing it, celebrate it, unleash it on the world.

Hang with people who appreciate you for who you are and don't want to change you. When you're yourself, you make the right friends.

Accept yourself. Don't focus on the flaws; no one is perfect. Embrace each and every thing about you that makes you unique.

Accept others. Don't be judgy if you don't want others to judge you. My mom always told me if you don't have something nice to say, then don't say it. Sounds simple, but so true.

Never dress to impress. If all the girls wear pink on Wednesday, you wear blue! Don't follow the fashion of the crowd if it's not your style. Don't follow fads; start your own trend.

Don't compare yourself to others. Everyone has his or her individual strengths and weaknesses. You're not your best friend, and he or she isn't you. Don't waste time trying to measure up to others; set the bar for yourself.

Get a goal. Having a purpose helps you stay true to yourself and not cave when others try to make you conform.

You can't please everyone. This is my number one argument against trying to fit in. No matter what you do, no matter how hard you try, you will never make *everyone* happy. Not everyone will like you, and that's okay. There will always be one person (or several) who will tell you you're doing things all wrong just so they can control or belittle you. Make yourself happy and never apologize.

#askAriel

My friend loves to make fun of my clothes. She literally greets me with "What are you wearing?" I keep telling her to quit it but she won't.

You may not be able to control what she says, but you can certainly control how you react to it. Obviously, you're bothered by her criticism and she knows it—it's fueling her to keep going. Don't be bothered. Ignore her snide remarks. Your style is your style, and no one has a right to tell you how to dress. Also, consider what kind of friend this person is—why is she putting you down? Is that really a good friend? Give her the cold shoulder when she talks to you that way and maybe she'll take the hint.

I am totally into astronomy and kids in my school think I'm weird. What should I do?

Find a group or club that loves constellations and space

as much as you do. Guess what? To them, your passion for planets isn't weird, it's wonderful. Some people in your school may not understand what you're about or appreciate it, and it's not your job to fix that. My parents always told me to "find my tribe," meaning surround yourself with like-minded people who enjoy doing what you do. It may take a while, but know that they're out there and when you find them, you'll feel at home. Hang in there—and for the record, I think astronomy is fascinating.

My friend is pressuring me to get my ears pierced (she has three piercings in each ear). I'm not sure I want to (it kind of scares me), but she says I'll be the only one in high school who doesn't have her ears pierced.

You don't have to do something that makes you uncomfortable—period. I seriously doubt you will be the only one without holes in her ears, and frankly, it's your choice to make, not hers, thank you very much. Your friend isn't being a very good friend if she doesn't respect your hesitation. Why does she even care? Is she looking out for you? Trying to upgrade your accessorizing? Or is she just trying to control you or make you feel like an outcast? If you're not sure how you'll like the look of earrings, then get some clip-ons and give them a try before you do anything.

If and when you're ready to pierce your ears, I promise you it's no big deal. But if I were you, I would take your mom to the mall to do it—not your friend. I'm not sure she has your best interests at heart.

I'm being cyberbullied and I'm scared that if I tell, it will only make things worse.
That's what the bully is counting on—that you are so afraid of him or her that you will just sit there and take it. Bullies manipulate and try to get inside your head so you're too intimidated to tell on them. Stop the silence and end this now. You need to alert an adult about what's going on immediately. Don't try to handle this on your own and don't think that by doing so you'll make things worse. I promise you, it can only make things better. It will only get worse if you say nothing and allow fear to rule your life.

Someone wrote some mean comments about my friend's YouTube video, and I didn't stick up for her. I feel really bad, but is it my job to get involved? Shouldn't I mind my own business?
To an extent, you mind your own business. But if this is a good friend and you know they're going through something, I think you're obligated to stand up for them. I know I would do this for my best friends and they would

do it (and have done it) for me. You don't necessarily have to pick a fight with the person posting negative comments. Just post something positive like "Love this video!" to counteract the negativity. Encourage your friend to ignore the haters and keep going with what makes her happy. Just don't pretend like nothing is happening. If you love and care about her, you owe it to her to back her up.

Build your squad

If you're one of my people (and you know who you are), I would seriously trust you with my life. If we were on the *Titanic,* I know you'd save me a seat in the lifeboat next to you and vice versa. Friends like that are hard to come by. They are your safety net, your cheering section, your sanity in an otherwise crazy world. These are the people who will build you up when others try to tear you down. They believe in you and love you for who you are, even your flaws. In fact, they love you *more* for your flaws because they see them as what makes you special. I count my family in my squad—my parents and brother always have my back. Beyond that, I have a few friends who are always there for me and would fight for me fiercely. I don't have to ask; they would come to my defense in a heartbeat and have on several occasions. Where do you find people like this? I wish I could tell you; I seriously lucked out. But what I will say is that they're worth searching for and when you find them, you'll know.

I think the beauty of friendship is that each person represents a unique relationship and fills different needs. My dad once told me that the people in your life are like the parts of a tree. Some are like leaves—they'll be in your life for maybe only a season. Others are like branches or twigs—they might come to you a little later on and stay for a while, but they may eventually break away. And others are the trunk—they are a part of who you are and will always be. They are your strength and your support, and you grow because of them. The key is to value everyone who comes into your life, no matter when and no matter how long they stay. They appear in your life for a reason, and hopefully it's to help you grow and discover who you are and want to be.

It's not often you meet someone far from home who you never realized lived right beside you. Daniel Skye is one of those people I believe I would have met at some point in my life regardless of my social media career. Why? Because I just can't picture my life without him. Before I was asked to headline a tour, Digi asked me to guest on a couple of stops to see how it would go. On one of my first guest appearances, I met Daniel backstage. We hit it off right away and discovered we both lived in South Florida just fifteen minutes away from each other! Fast-forward and one day when we were back home, his mom texted mine and invited us to come over for Shabbat dinner. Since then our parents have become friends, and Daniel and I have gotten really close. I consider him one of my best friends and someone I can trust with my deepest thoughts.

He is the person I call when I need a shoulder to cry on. When I need to talk something through, I trust he will always listen carefully and give me the best advice, without judging. I feel comfortable discussing religion, philosophy, and my deepest fears with him. He's the kind of friend who will drop everything he's doing and come over to give me a hug when I need one, no questions asked. Not only do we live just fifteen minutes away from one another in Florida, but his house and my apartment in LA are that close as well! I consider myself extremely lucky to have a friend who is on such a similar path. Because his music career began a few years before mine, he has a lot of insight about the music business and writing and recording. Some of my favorite sessions have been in the recording studio in his backyard in LA. Yup, Skye is a definite keeper.

Another person I could not live without is Arii. She and I met in sixth grade at a time in my life when I was more about having a big gang of friends than a small, tight-knit group. There were seven of us, but she and I really clicked. She was always coming over after school, hanging out, and we shared an obsession for Jordans. I can't tell you how many times we waited in lines for hours at stores trying to score a pair of these shoes! As time went on, she stayed by me while others kind of drifted away. My dad always warned me that people grow up and grow apart. I went on tour and was traveling for two months, and when I came back, things were different. Arii was still my best friend, but some of the other friends in my group treated me like an outsider. Somehow in those eight weeks, I'd changed and evolved; my head was a different place, and they'd gone on without me. I no longer "fit" with them.

I remember one particularly upsetting conversation, when one of my "close friends" asked me out of the blue, "So, when are you gonna stop this whole social media thing?"

My jaw literally hit the floor. Excuse me? That's like asking me, "So, when do you think you'll stop breathing?" I honestly didn't know what to say. I was really taken aback.

I thought she understood how important this was to me. I thought she understood *me*.

"Um, what do you mean?" Maybe I'd misheard her. Maybe she hadn't meant to come off sounding as obnoxious as she did. Maybe she was suffering from a head trauma.

She shrugged. "I mean, it's fun for now, but you know it's gonna end tomorrow."

Thanks for the vote of confidence! Like, COME FOR MY NECK, DANG!! Now I was getting pissed: "No, I don't think it will end tomorrow, because it's what I love to do. And I always want to be doing what I love."

"Well, I think it's kind of weird," she continued. "But, whatever." Just like that, she turned her back on me and walked away.

That night, I tossed and turned and replayed the conversation over and over again in my head. Where did this come from? Why was she suddenly being so negative? And if this is what my supposed BFF really thought, was she my BFF after all? Honestly, I expected more from her. I expected her to know that this passion was my priority and to not discourage me from following my dreams. I felt betrayed and stabbed in the back, and I had to face the facts: my friend was no friend, she was a frenemy.

Needless to say, I cut her out of my life pretty quickly. Does anyone really need that negativity in her life? I didn't even want to know what brought it on (my guess is jealousy and insecurity), but when someone tries to dull your sparkle and make you doubt yourself, it's "adios, amiga" time.

So I really had to rebuild my squad, figure out who did and didn't have my back, and pick and choose carefully the people I put my trust in. Arii was one of those people. In a way, nobody truly gets me or my life like she does. She was there with me before musical.ly, and she's been on this ride with me ever since. We both got on musical.ly at the same time and our videos got featured within weeks of each other. I remember at that time, haters on social media created "Ariel vs. Arii" pages not even realizing we knew each other and were close friends. Of course, in classic Arii fashion, she had a plan to right this wrong! We decided to do a musical.ly collab to "Dreams and Nightmares" by Meek Mill and that was the end of that rumor. Pretty soon, we were doing meet and greets together, going to DigiFest together, and taking trips to LA together.

I remember on our first LA trip, we decided to go to the Santa Monica Pier and ride the Ferris wheel. We tweeted it out a few hours beforehand to see if anybody would show up and ride with us. When we got there, there were literally hundreds of people waiting to hang out with us. It was incredible! We gave them hugs, took selfies, and made musical.lys with our fans for six hours straight. There we were, two kids from Pembroke Pines, Florida, having this incredible experience together.

Arii's the first one I text to approve of my outfit of the day, and the first person I call for advice. After a session in the recording studio, I play her my music first to see what she thinks, and I trust her judgment because she knows me—really, really knows me. No matter what, she's got my back, and I hope she knows I've got hers. I still get a lot of strange and random hate from people who are in the social media world, and usually I'll ignore it and move on. But not Arii: she'll defend me and stand up for me. Everyone should have a friend who is their ride-or-die—Arii is mine, even if that ride can get a little crazy at times. Don't get me wrong, she's a good driver. But the girl has some serious road rage. If someone tries to cut her off, look out, she will take their head off! But if there is one person I want driving down this road with me, it is her.

MY BRAVE BROTHER, JACOB

My brother may be younger than I am, but it doesn't stop me from looking up to him. Jacob has always been uniquely himself, but one of the things that inspires me most about him is how confident he is and how little he cares about what other people think of him. When Jacob was in elementary school, he went through a stage where he enjoyed painting his fingernails. When I had my girlfriends over doing a spa day, Jacob always wanted to join in. We never thought much about it; it was just something Jacob enjoyed. My parents never put any boundaries on us in terms of gender norms. If Jacob wanted to play with princess dolls and wear pink socks, so be it. All of Jacob's best friends since he was in preschool have been girls anyway, so it seemed natural when he started wearing nail polish and playing dress up and wanting to paint his room pink. Even though it seemed natural to us and, luckily, to most of the people in our community and inner circle, there are always people who don't like different and want everyone to fit into a specific box. Every year at our elementary school we had a book fair and Mom would take us after school to pick out some books. One year a boy came up to Jacob and said, "Ewww, you're gross! Boys don't wear nail polish! You're stupid." My mom and I overheard, and Mom immediately sprang into mama-bear mode. She was ready to pounce and give this boy a piece of her mind. But Jacob stopped her and said, "We both know who the stupid one is, Mom." I'll never forget that image of my little brother, just seven years old, completely unbothered. Makes me smile. And I'm still proud to this day.

Two years ago on Christmas Eve, we were in the car headed to my grandma Lita's house for Christmas dinner.

Troye Sivan's song "Heaven" was playing, my parents were talking in the front seat, I was Snapchatting some friends, and suddenly Jacob, out of nowhere says, "I'm gay." His cheeks were flushed, and it was obvious he had been crying and we all fell silent. My dad stopped the car at the next red light and we all immediately told him how much we loved him and how proud of him we were. But as quickly as he mentioned it, he made it clear that he was done talking about it and didn't want us to talk about it, either. It was a very profound moment and we stayed quiet the rest of the ride in respect of his wishes. It took some time before he was ready to talk to us about it again, and another year before he came out publicly on social media. As usual, Jacob did it in typical Jacob fashion. He had posted a photo of himself wearing an "Empower Women" cutoff T-shirt on Instagram and he began to receive comments like, "Are you gay?" and "Isn't that a girl's shirt?" and Jacob began to respond to the questions with one simple word: "Yes." In this unassuming way, Jacob let people know what he had known for a very long time. I respect him so much for his courage and I am proud of the example he is for other kids, specifically the LGBTQ youth. Needless to say, I feel blessed to have him as my brother.

10 TYPES OF "FRIENDS" WHO AREN'T WORTH YOUR TIME

If you know these people, I highly recommend reevaluating your relationship. They're not good for you and if you stay in their circle, they'll only bring you down.

1. The Possessive Pal: This friend wants you all to him- or herself. They are very insecure about you having other friends; this can be stifling and unhealthy.

2. The Self-Absorbed Friend: The one who only wants to talk about herself. She never lets you get a word in. It's always "me, me, me." We all know that one person who ONLY talks about themselves, even when you are having a problem. This friend will always turn it around to make it about themselves, not you. Scenario: you spot your boyfriend holding another girl's hand in the hallway. When you run to her for consolation, Miss Self-Absorbed says, "You think that's bad?" and tells you a sob story about her boyfriend breaking up with her last summer. Um, wasn't she supposed to be listening to YOU?

3. The Bad Influence: This friend is always thinking up new ways to break the rules and get you to join in. The pal who pressures you to party, cheat, or do other things you're against. "Relax," she tells you, "you won't get in trouble." Famous last words!

4. The Underminer: You get a B+ on your test and you're thrilled, and she is there to remind you that if you had studied harder you would have gotten an A like her.

5. The Criticizer: This so-called friend knows everything about everything (don't try to argue with her) and criticizes you for doing anything that strays from the way she would do it. She's right; you're wrong. Period.

6. The Debbie Downer: Woe is her—and she will whine and cry on your shoulder any chance she gets. Stay away from negative people; they suck the life out of you! Literally, I can be in a great mood, and as soon as I spend time with a negative person, my energy is zapped and I'm left feeling drained!

7. The Boy-Crazy Bud: You know her, the friend who dumps you the minute a boyfriend is in the picture, makes a plan with you but backs out if he asks her to do something instead. Ariel who? She focuses solely on her BF until the relationship is over and done—then she wants to be your friend again because her calendar is wide open!

8. The Passive-Aggressive Pal: She knows how to hurt you and where you are most vulnerable, and she finds ways to get in her jabs verbally with a smile on her face. This so-called pal has perfected the snarky compliment disguised as an insult, i.e., "I love how you never care what your hair looks like! It must make it so much easier to get ready for school every day!" She will say something obnoxious and hurtful, then tell you you're being way too sensitive.

9. The Attention Grabber: She has to be queen bee, dictating and controlling what you do and when you do it. She always has to be the center of attention or watch out, she will lash out at everyone around her. Why does it feel like you

have a leash around your neck whenever she's around?

10. The User: She uses you for everything from class notes and homework assignments to lunch money and borrowing clothes. The more you give in, the more she'll take advantage. She looks at you and sees "sucker."

Story Time

WHEN MATTHEW MET ARIEL

Funny story: Matthew actually came to Arii's and my first meet and greet. Go off Matthew, we stan. He was a fan! But a few months earlier, when we were just starting on musical.ly, my mom discovered him while reading comments on our videos. My brother had made a musical.ly, and someone wrote, "Oh, you're so dumb and you look gay." Well, my brother is gay, but at the time he wasn't out, and while the word "gay" is not an insult, it was obvious the intention of the person was to be rude. It was a hurtful remark for a young kid who was just trying to be creative and express himself. Matthew actually commented back, slamming the hater on Jacob's behalf: "Stop coming for him, what's wrong with being gay? There's nothing wrong with it, you need to shut up!" My mom read what he wrote and fell instantly in love with him. She commented back a thank-you and showed Jacob and me his remark. About a month later, Matthew's mom, Julie, who is now like a second mom to me, reached out to my mom and told her she was going to fly Matthew out for Arii's and my upcoming meet and greet as a surprise. We only knew him from messaging back and forth a bit, so it was a really amazing moment to meet him in person.

I remember he had these big, round glasses and he gave me the biggest hug. And when I thanked him for having my brother's back, he just shrugged and smiled at me: "No biggie." To him it was no big deal; he was just doing what he thought was right. He has a ginormous heart, and like my other best friends, he will spring into superhero mode if anyone hates on me or my family.

We followed each other on Instagram, exchanged numbers, started texting and DMing, and it just really went on from there. He was a fan who evolved into a best, best, best friend. Since then, he's started doing makeup videos and pursuing social media himself, which is great because it's something we both love and share. And we're both growing, and expanding our horizons at the same time—me into music, him into makeup. He moved out to LA, so now I see him whenever I'm there. We're also both a little obsessed with our long nails. It's really funny how people come into your life unexpectedly, yet you can't help feeling "this was meant to be."

Baby Steps

HOW TO BREAK UP WITH A BFF

I'm not going to lie to you: cutting ties with a former best friend isn't easy. Friendships tend to feel more forever than some guy you've been dating a few months who turned out to be a jerk. At first, it can be hard to picture your life without your friend intensely in it; you have so much history. You may be tempted to backpedal, but if the relationship has turned toxic, it's time to rip the Band-Aid off . . . 'cause it's RIP to this friendship! . . . GET IT?! I KNOW YOU LAUGHED!

Be honest. Explain how you're feeling and why it's not working for you anymore, i.e., "I don't think we have as much in common as we used to" or "I don't feel like I can trust you" or "I don't like how you've been treating me." Stay calm and cool, but also direct—you want to give clarity and closure.

Put some space between you. Once you've expressed your desire to end the friendship, don't call or text or Snap and continue to discuss it. Resist the urge to stalk her Instagram story and comment with emoji hearts; those days are done. The idea is to separate; you can't keep your lives tightly woven together. If she insists on clinging and trying to patch things up, I'd still recommend taking some downtime. It's possible that you two might be friends in the future, but right now, you need time off.

Move on. Actually do it! Make new friends, discover new interests, explore new places. Above all, don't feel bad about doing something that needed to be done. You cut a negative person out of your life. It might feel weird at first; you might find yourself reminiscing about the good ol' days when things were *actually* good. Okay, I'll let you have a few days to register the loss; then I'm going to give you some tough love: time to get on with your life.

#AskAriel

My friend refuses to let me follow her finsta. What's up with that?

Finsta is a tricky subject. I have a finsta with just five followers because I want only my closest inner circle of friends to see those posts. If this is a friend who you consider your best friend, then that's an issue, but if he or she is more of an acquaintance, then maybe there are some things on there that they don't want you to see for whatever reason. This may feel hurtful to you, but you have to respect their feelings. Consider who you allow on your private account and recognize there are a lot of people you won't allow in either. For me, I consider finsta like a small group chat with my best friends. I don't even want my brother on my finsta, and I obviously love him and am extremely close with him. It's nothing against anyone and it shouldn't be taken personally. Now, if you are super close to this person and feel they are shutting you out, ask them about it and say, "Hey, you're not accepting me on your finsta. Did I do something? Is there something I should know?" They should be able to give you a straight-up answer, but you need to be prepared for an honest (and maybe hurtful) answer. They may say they simply don't feel as close to you as you may feel toward them. It's a tough pill to swallow, but should at least let you know where you stand and give you an answer about your friendship going forward.

My friends text me at all hours of the night. Is it rude to tell them I need to sleep?

No, it's not rude. You don't know how many times I've done this to my friends. I get home really late at night, totally exhausted, and they start texting me nonstop. What do I do? I say, "Guys, I'm going to sleep. Love you lots. Talk tomorrow. Good night." If these are your friends, they will understand that you need your beauty sleep.

My BFF has made new friends in school and she wants to hang with them instead of me. I don't know what to do.

I've drifted with friends before, and a lot of the time it happens naturally: You're best friends with someone for years; then you develop new interests and bond with other people who share them. Sometimes as you grow up, you grow in different directions. It doesn't mean you don't care about each other. It might just mean you're each learning who you are, and maybe some of her new friends have interests that are closer to what she's interested in right now. If she's not being rude to you, it's possible that she is simply a little preoccupied—I wouldn't overthink it. Your friendship could easily pick up down the road. Let her do her thing and you do yours. But if it's really upsetting you, then talk to her. Ask her, "What's happening? I feel kind of left out of your life. Did I do something to make you mad?" If she says no, then it is time to move on and find other friends who appreciate you and want to spend time with you. I promise you, they're out there and they're lucky to have you!

My friends from school never seem to like or comment on my Instagram posts—I think it's rude. Should I confront them?

I'm gonna give you some tough love here. I think if you confront them, it's just going to make it awkward between you guys, and they're going to feel like you're begging. My suggestion is to put up posts that you're proud of, things that you want to share. People will start liking them for the right reasons—because you're being genuine—not because you asked for a like. And if your friends still refuse to like or comment, *and* they are liking other people's posts . . . well, you know where I stand on this. Friends support friends and lift them up. If yours aren't doing that for you, then think carefully about who you choose to include in your inner circle.

GREEN is the color of life. It reminds me of how you should always be grateful for all you have and appreciate each day you're given.

9

A helping hand

Part of becoming a woman in the eyes of the Jewish faith is doing a charitable act. For my bat mitzvah project, I visited the Susan B. Anthony Recovery Center in Fort Lauderdale. My mom had been volunteering there for as long as I can remember, and she finally took me and my brother when we were old enough to understand what it was about. It's a facility full of kind, loving, caring people; a residential space for pregnant women and mothers with children to stay while being treated for a drug and/or alcohol addiction. It makes recovery a lot less stressful because they are allowed to live alongside their children and don't have to worry that their kids will wind up in foster care. It's become a part of our family and something we do together, so it became my mitzvah project. I remember we brought books and toys and stuffed animals and spent a whole day reading to the kids and playing with them. On the way home, I didn't say much—I had to let it sink in a little. And you know me, I am *never* quiet, but I was honestly so moved by the experience. It touched me on such a deep level. I could not believe how different these kids' lives were from mine, and it made me appreciate how lucky I am and how I rarely even *think* about all I take for granted and all I've been blessed with. I have so much to be grateful for, especially a family that loves and supports my dreams wholeheartedly.

That night, I journaled about it, not only what I saw, but the feelings I took away from that day. Every time I made a kid laugh or smile, it literally made my heart happy. My mom will tell you it's a gift to be able to do that, and when you have a gift, it's your responsibility to use it. We were brought up to believe that charity doesn't always mean giving monetary gifts; giving of your time with love and energy is just as important and often more powerful. My life is pretty crazy busy, and there are days I feel overwhelmed with work and stressed out because there just aren't enough hours to do everything. But it dawned on me that that's exactly when I need a little reminder, a little reality check. When I take time out to help others, I find myself. All the stuff that's extra and unimportant will eventually fade away, and I tune into my purpose and why I do what I do: to bring joy into people's lives.

Another time, my friend Charles and I visited a community home for troubled girls who have been abused or neglected, or are going through some kind of crisis. This time I didn't bring gifts. We just got some chairs and sat around with a small group of girls in a circle, sharing our thoughts and answering questions.

They wanted to know how I got started in social media and how I decided what videos to make.

"I pretty much talk about what's going on in my life," I explained. "And stuff that I like to do. You can make a video about anything. What do you all like to do?"

One girl's hand went up: "I do rainbow loom bracelets."

She wasn't kidding! She was really good at them and knew how to do cool patterns I'd never even seen before.

"I think you could start your own rainbow loom channel on YouTube!" I told her.

Her face lit up; she loved that idea. It was like I'd given her permission to be herself. Other girls showed us their sketchbooks filled with these amazing drawings. I was so impressed with their talent and creativity, and I really hated to leave. I felt like I was just starting to get through to them, and I could see the smiles spreading around the room and feel their confidence building. All they needed was one person to believe in them, to say, "Yeah, you can do it! Go for it!" I talk a lot about self-confidence, but I also think everyone needs someone, even if it's only one person like your parent or a teacher or a coach, who believes in you and encourages you to reach for the stars. Or in this girl's case, to reach for the rainbow.

VOLUNTEER

Story Time
THE TRUTH

I'm constantly reminded how precious life truly is and how it can change in a split second. You see it in nature, when the trees suddenly go from a blooming, vibrant green to drying up and shedding their leaves. And I see it lately in my grandparents getting older. It's not something I talk about often; I hate for my fans to see me not being happy. But just recently, I made a video in the midst of a total meltdown because I wanted to be 100 percent honest. I know people expect me to be funny, to make light of a situation and joke about it. But in this one moment, I was just feeling really vulnerable. I'm a teenage girl; we have our days when we get all weepy and bent out of shape for no apparent reason except, well, we're teenagers.

So here's the truth, all of it. It's not like I was purposely keeping it a secret; it's just very hard for me to talk about without getting emotional. Putting it out there makes it real, which I wish it wasn't. My mom's dad has Parkinson's disease and is declining, and her mom has MSA (multiple system atrophy), a rare neurodegenerative disorder. Both need assistance in getting around; Papa uses a walker and Safta is in a wheelchair. They can no longer do the basic daily routines we all take for granted and they require a caregiver 24/7. We went through several agencies before finding the perfect match for my grandparents, a lovely angel of a lady we all adore, named Bethina, who, coincidentally, lives down the street from them. While my mom's parents have been struggling for years with degenerative diseases, my father's parents, Lito and Lita seemed to be doing okay, but late last year my Lito was diagnosed with stage-four lung cancer. He went to the hospital to have the tumor removed, but never recovered. He was in and out of the hospital and hospice for about three months before he died, and although it's completely unrealistic, a part of me just thought he'd always be there. His passing was the first time I had to deal with the reality and finality of death. Even though I know people die, I never allowed myself to believe that anyone close to me actually would.

Despite all my grandparents' struggles with illness, I will not allow myself to forget memories of them at better times. To me, they are these full-of-life people with boundless energy and more love and patience then you could ever imagine. I think of Lita as the best hugger in the world—not someone who has knee problems and struggles to walk. My brain just doesn't want to accept that they may not recover and bounce back, and I've really been wrestling with my feelings. As a family, we talk about what it means to age and how it's difficult to accept that sometimes, getting older can mean getting sick and suffering. But you never want to see the people you love hurt. It hurts me. It scares me. It makes me wish I could edit life as easily as I edit a video: pause, rewind, cut out everything but the good stuff.

When I was a toddler and my parents were working, my mom's mother was my babysitter. Safta never sat still so we were always out and about, "gallivanting" as she called it. When I got older I would go to their house after school and help her bake and do my homework. Safta is an amazing photographer and artist, and when I was younger, we would take pictures together for hours. We would shop for props and cute outfits and stage these intricate photo shoots with me posing and glamming it up as she snapped away. Many of the throwback photos you see on my Instagram were taken by her. She also paints, and her home had this huge art studio. I remember walking in there and seeing paint brushes, palettes, and canvases everywhere. She'd be intently working on painting a sunset or a still life, but as soon as she heard my footsteps, she'd get excited and hurry me over to proudly show me her work and ask me all about my day. She even had a small easel set up for me to paint alongside her. I used to know how to speak Hebrew, and she would always speak it to me—it was like our secret language. We have a lot of little inside things between us, like every time I go on vacation, she will take my hand and remind me to be safe: "Ariel, you do not leave your mother's side. You don't talk to strangers. If you need to go somewhere, you take your mother or father with you. Understand?" It made perfect sense to tell me this when I was five, but now I'm seventeen and she still gave me this speech a few weeks ago before my trip to NYC! Then she'll add, "Send me pictures. Take lots of pictures." I always do, because I know how much photos mean to her, and I realize she's in a wheelchair these days and can't get around much, so I have to make sure she doesn't feel like she's missing out.

My Papa is the funniest. After Shabbat dinner, it's always time for one of his jokes—he still cracks me and my brother up (now you know where I get my jokes from). He could have easily been a stand-up comedian or a YouTube sensation. The stories of him as a kid in Cuba are hysterical. One of my favorites is from when he was about twelve years old. He and his friends would sit next to people on the bus and just start barking and growling under their breath until all the passengers were afraid to get near them! Eventually the bus driver had enough and would kick him and his friends off the bus and tell them not to come back. It's funny to think our grandparents were once mischievous little kids, too, just trying to pass the time and have fun. I encourage you to talk to your older relatives and ask them to share stories about their lives. You may be surprised at what you learn! It will give you a fuller picture about how they came to be the person they are today and may even answer questions about traits you have that have been passed down through the generations.

When we were younger, Papa and Jacob and I would build these enormous block towers that we would keep up for weeks at a time. I remember intricate rooms and garages where we would park our tiny matchbox cars. We'd also play games, dominos being Papa's favorite from his childhood in Cuba; I've never been able to beat him and I strongly suggest you never try! A few years ago, when Safta was first diagnosed with MSA, they decided to sell their house, which was too big for just the two of them, and moved closer to our house so my mom could go over if they needed help. I make it a point to see them as often as possible and to say "I love you" as much as I can. Because one day, I won't be able to tell them that, and I want them to know how much they mean to me, and how much I appreciate how they've been there for me in good times and not-so-good times. I want to be there for them. If you remember, I was in their home when I made my first musical.ly, and my grandma still watches my videos faithfully; she's my number one fan. I don't think she quite gets the whole social media, live your life out loud thing, but she'll say, "Ariel, that scene of you on the stairs was beautiful!"

So yeah, this Story Time wasn't a barrel of laughs (sorry!). But I hope you know it came from my heart, and it's important for me to say it and for you to hear it. I'm learning more and more every day how the connections we make between us as human beings are the most important things we can create in our lives. Reach out wherever and whenever you can, to people you love, and to people you don't know yet. They all need kindness and understanding. The love you put out there will always come back to you— my Safta told me that, and for the record, she's never, ever wrong.

Baby Steps
CURL UP AND WATCH A MOVIE

I've grown up watching movies my whole life. And I love all kinds of movies. But when I'm feeling blue, there's nothing quite like sitting down with a favorite snack and watching a great love story with talented actors who will make you laugh and cry. I grab some white cheddar popcorn, brew a cup of chamomile tea with honey, cuddle with Bleu, pull my white cotton throw blanket over us, and watch one of these:

1. *Love, Rosie*
2. *When Harry Met Sally*
3. *Titanic*
4. *The Notebook*
5. *Keith*
6. *Grease*
7. *A Walk to Remember*
8. *The Fault in Our Stars*
9. *10 Things I Hate About You*
10. *Sixteen Candles*

#askAriel

All I hear about lately is global warming and climate change and it's got me really worried. What can I do to help?

First of all, it's great that you care and want to do something about it. I always hear the expression "Think global. Act local." That means, don't try to fix the whole world—start in your own backyard. Find little things you can do in your home, your neighborhood, and your community to make a difference in the environment. Make sure you recycle, don't leave water running or lights turned on. Talk to your family about things you can to do together, and join an environmental group at school. You'll be making a difference, and I bet you'll make some great new friends!

There's this homeless guy I always see on my walk to

school. I feel really bad for him. Should I try to help?
I'm really proud of you for noticing someone in need because not everyone would. Too many people would just walk past, too absorbed in their own lives to ever see the problems that exist in their own backyard. If you want to help, I think the way to start is tell your parents or a teacher. Because you don't know this man, it's probably not a good idea to engage with him alone. Even though your heart is in the right place, you need to be safe. Ask an adult to go with you—maybe you can bring him some food or blankets or clothing. Or contact a homeless shelter or organization in your community and let them know you've seen someone who needs support and you want to help make a difference. Good for you!

My dad just got laid off from his job and I feel so awful for him! I don't know what to say or do to make him feel better.
Your dad is going through a tough time and it may not be an easy problem for him to fix or something you can help him with. He may feel sad, mad, even ashamed, so just be there for him and let him know he has your love and support. If he wants to talk about it, be a good listener. Give him a huge hug and suggest some fun things you can do together to get his mind off things. Above all, try not to

worry! It's really hard to see your parent hurting; we expect them to be superdad and supermom, and sometimes we forget they're just human. Your dad will get through this, especially if he knows he has you in his cheering section.

10

Puppy love

Animals love you so completely, and they ask for nothing in return but for you to love them back. Anyone who has ever had a pet will tell you that, and I can't imagine how life would've been without my two dogs, Murphy and Bleu. They complete me!

I grew up with "Murphy Monster" and she was our pet from the time I was born. I got to love her, cuddle, and play with her for sixteen years and I couldn't be more grateful for the time we had together. How she came into my parents' lives is another moment of serendipity that seems to be our family's pattern. My mom was a theater actor who would often support her friends and see their shows. One night, she and my dad (they weren't even married yet) went to catch a friend in an opening night performance. During intermission, they were discussing how much they both wanted a dog, and that their ideal dog would be a mix between a rottweiler and a Labrador. The box office manager overheard their conversation and said she had a rescue puppy at home that fit that exact description! She told my parents she would be back after act 3 with the puppy.

When the play ended and my parents were heading out, the manager had indeed returned with the dog and, of course, my mother fell in love with her instantly. The rest is Martin family history. Murphy was likely neither a rottweiler nor a Lab; she looked more like a German shepherd mix who never grew up, but she was the sweetest, most loving mutt anyone could ever hope for. My mom told me she was very protective of me when I was born and would sleep beside my crib every night. She would assess strangers before they got too close and growl at them to back off if she didn't like the looks of them. But truth be told, we all believed that if a robber broke into the house, Murphy was more likely to lick them to death than attack them. She was just such a gentle soul. Living in South Florida on a lake, we had our share of wildlife—iguanas, ducks, lizards, and frogs—showing up as visitors. While other dogs would chase and eat them, Murphy simply wanted to play. She looked so rejected when the ducks would run away from her, terrified. Her eyes seemed to plead, "Come back! I won't bite!"

Around the time Murphy turned fifteen, she started to deteriorate and it broke my heart. She had already survived a heatstroke two years earlier and a surgery to remove a large tumor, but she was growing frail. It had become more difficult for her to even stand on her own and she began to bump into things, unable to see due to her cataracts. In the summer of 2015, while I was away on tour with my dad, my mom made the difficult decision to let Murphy go. She had been holding out hope for her to survive until we got back to say goodbye, but she just couldn't watch her suffer anymore. As much as I would have loved to give her one last hug, I know Mom did the right thing by putting her out of her misery and pain. But I will always miss her.

If ever a dog could be the opposite of Murphy, it's Bleu! While Murphy was stout and muscular with dark brown fur and an unassuming personality, Bleu is a six-pound white puffball of energy who thinks she's the boss. Actually, she kind of *is* the boss in our family! It took some time after Murphy died to convince my parents to get another dog. They were very adamant that it was NOT going to happen.

Our lives were too busy, we traveled too much, we were never home. There was absolutely no way we could get another dog. Then, one day, Jacob and I asked my mom if we could go to a puppy store that also had rescues, "just to look." My mom is a sucker for babies: humans, dogs, even reptiles! So, I knew if we went "just to look," I'd probably be able to convince her to take one home. It didn't take long for us to each find a puppy we felt attached to. Mom was holding a boxer, Jacob had a dachshund, and I found a Maltipoo. Pretty soon, Mom was actually considering getting ALL three dogs. Then my father showed up and reality set in.

"We're not getting three dogs," he told us. "We're not even getting one." He knew when my mom called him to come to the store that he was in for an argument from all of us.

But it was too late; our hearts had all turned to mush and Jacob and I knew that we were going home with a new addition to the family.

We started thinking about logistics: we needed to get a dog we could travel with—that meant no to the boxer because he was already pretty big and heavy. We also needed a hypoallergenic dog because my dad tends to have allergic reactions to short-haired dogs. I looked at the Maltipoo—whom I had already named Bleu—and she was the clear winner. "You're coming home with us!" I told her as I cuddled her in my arms. "Look how sweet she is—and so calm."

She yapped in agreement and my dad rolled his eyes. "Calm, huh?"

"Calm—but fun," I improvised. I was so, so in love with her. "Dad," I begged. "She's my baby! She's only two months old. She's my dog, I know it. I feel this strong connection and I can't leave her. I'll take care of her. I'll clean up her poop! Dad, how can you say no to this face?"

Well, he couldn't. Once he held her and she nibbled his finger . . . that was it. Love at first bite. Bleu became a Martin in March 2017, and she has brightened our lives in so many unexpected ways. Because we split our time between Florida and LA, the intention was to take her with us—she'd be a bicoastal pup. But something interesting began to happen. Growing up, my mom wasn't allowed to have a dog. Safta was always terribly afraid of dogs and thought they would make a mess of her pristine home. She would never even allow Murphy into her house! But Bleu changed all that. You know how they say people don't change, and as you get older you get more set in your ways? Well, in this case, Bleu broke those rules—she completely changed my Safta's mind. Not only has our little dog been welcomed into my grandparents' home, but she has become a part of their lives and is very therapeutic for them. She brings so much joy to my Safta and Papa, so we now let her stay with them and Bethina when we travel. I think Bleu is the luckiest dog alive because she has three homes, four moms (my mom, me, Safta, and Bethina), and a best friend, a dachshund named Movado that lives at Bethina's house with her daughter Lydia. Bleu gives all of us an endless supply of love and she gets the same in return—plus more than a few treats. We spoil her rotten. She's been the star of several of my videos including one where we bought practically the entire pet store so she felt comfy in her new home! She even has her own Instagram: @BabyBleuMartin. But I'm not sure who's luckier—her or us.

Baby Steps

HOW TO PROVE TO YOUR PARENTS YOU'RE READY FOR A PET

Okay, my dad was a tough sell on this: "Ariel, we travel so much. What will you do with the dog then? Who's going to walk her? Take care of her? Clean up after her? Are you thinking this through?"

"I am and I will!" I promised. "I'll do it all."

Then he cheerfully reminded me how many goldfish I *had* to have that had bitten the dust because I got bored of them.

"This is different!" I insisted. "This puppy will be my baby."

If your parents are still not buying it, then try the following:

• **Do your homework.** Research the type of pet

you want and anticipate all of your mom's and dad's concerns *before* they voice them: "I know you're worried about a dog shedding—this dog doesn't shed and is a hundred percent hypoallergenic!" Or "I know you think hamsters are a lot of work, but I'll keep it in my room and you'll never have to lift a finger!"

- **Be practical.** If you live in a tiny apartment, you can't get a huge Lab or a 120-pound Akita. Make sure the animal you're angling to get would work within your family's accommodations.

- **Elaborate on the plusses of pet ownership,** i.e., "People who own dogs lead happier and longer lives." Mention that having a dog will get you outdoors more often (and away from video games), and that a dog can protect and make your home feel more safe and secure. It's all win-win!

- **Explain how pets teach responsibility.** Just saying, if your parents want you to act more grown-up and mature, this is a perfect way to help that process along. You will vow to feed, walk, clean, and play with your pet and make that a priority in your life. Prove to your parents how responsible you can be in all sorts of little ways—do the dishes, help your little bro with his homework, offer to help your mom make dinner. The more you show how mature and willing to pitch in you are, the easier they'll be to convince.

- **Do a test run.** By this, I mean offer to watch a neighbor's or friend's pet for a weekend so both you and your parents can see what it's like and how you will handle it. You can even offer to walk dogs in your neighborhood. All of the above are good ways to break everyone into the idea of pet ownership and responsibility.

- **Don't give up.** My dad wasn't instantly convinced when Jacob and I started begging and pleading for a puppy. He had to slowly warm to the idea and it took weeks of us bringing it up and him and my mom saying no. Don't whine, throw a tantrum, or slam your door if your parents say no—this will get you nowhere. Understand their concerns and respect them, and just repeat the prior steps. Bleu was definitely worth all the effort and now none of us can imagine our lives without her.

#askAriel

I love your style! What are your favorite stores to shop in? Fave labels?

Nike . . . because they have Nike and Converse! Urban Outfitters, Puma, Foot Locker, Forever 21, Topshop, Zara. There's this online store called Fashion Nova and I get all my jeans there because most jeans don't have curves and theirs do. In terms of brands, I'm always on the lookout for Champion hoodies, Calvin Klein undies, and Nike sweatpants. I also love shopping in thrift shops for old distressed tees with lots of holes in them and jackets that no one else has.

Bra—yes or no?

No! Hell, no! Is that even a QUESTION? If I have a choice, no way. They're uncomfortable, they hurt, and I think any girl would agree with me on this.

One-piece or bikini?

I feel cuter in a bikini. My problem with one-pieces is that they don't hug me correctly. I'm not skinny-skinny; I'm a girl with curves, and I think it's hard to find the perfect one-piece that fits right on top as well as the hips and butt. Two-pieces are easier because you can also sometimes buy them as separates so the fit is perfection.

Your nails always look so cute—what are your favorite color polishes to wear?

I like baby shades: baby blue, baby pink, baby yellow, baby lavender. Soft pastels, I guess. I'm not a huge fan of dark colors unless I do black, which isn't very often. I don't match my nails with my outfits because sometimes I have my tips on for a month and a half, so I can't always coordinate my clothes with that. But I think that's okay: nails can have their very own color and personality and stand out.

When you sing the BLUES, you feel sad, down, and defeated. But here's the good news: you can and will bounce back. What doesn't break you makes you stronger.

I will survive

A few chapters ago, I shared my messy breakup with Boyfriend #2. Now it's time for full disclosure: two weeks after we both agreed it was over, done, *finito*, I called him. I know, I know—that is like rule number one for breakups: don't chase after him. What was I thinking? I'll tell you what I was thinking: I wanted to hear the sound of his voice. I wanted to talk to him. I wanted to feel that connection that had been so much a part of my life for almost a year. Clearly, I was not over him yet, and making that call just made things worse (which I knew it would). He didn't want to talk to me, which sent me into this horrendous self-pity spiral. It felt like my world was coming to an end. I literally felt so sad and missed him so much it was hard to function.

I was so depressed I decided to see a therapist to talk through my feelings. My parents were both very loving and supportive and gave me a few days to mope around the house and mourn. My dad said, "You know, this whole thing is like an open wound. If you go and you start picking at that wound while it's still open, you're never going to give it a chance to close. You have to take the time that you really need for yourself now and allow that wound to heal."

But by day 3, my mom decided it was time for me to get a grip (thanks, Sharon, you're a great lady)—this behavior was not helping matters and we were running out of tissues. She was determined to get me out of my pj's, off the couch, back to the land of the living. She sat down and looked me in the eye: "Okay, Ariel, enough is enough. You know what? We're going to wake up tomorrow, and we're going to go to the gym at eight in the morning. Then you're going to come back, do school for three hours, and practice driving for two hours." She gave me a game plan, something to focus on, a reason to get up in the morning and start living my life again. She told me, "It's time to get back to being you." Those words really sunk in. I'd lost my purpose, and when you lose who you are, you have to find yourself again.

One of my close friends, Josh, who's basically like a brother, insisted on picking me up the second he found out I was hurting. He drove us down to the beach at 11:00 one night, where we sat for hours talking about the happiest parts of our lives.

My best friend, Arii, was there for me the whole time, too. She slept over several nights in a row and we went out to eat, to the movies, shopping, driving—basically anything she could think of to just keep me busy and my mind off you-know-who. The distraction worked; I stopped sobbing over him and analyzing what went wrong. And once I did, the pieces of me that had been broken came back together again. Now I can look back and see the reality, not the fairy tale I thought our relationship was. I see where the red flags were and how I blindly ignored them.

Maybe some of you are reading this and nodding your heads: "Yup, I've been there. Breaking up is not just hard to do, it's *hell*." I won't argue with you on that, but I will tell you that it gets easier, a lot easier, and you get better at dealing with the aftermath. Several months past it, I feel like I'm Ariel again. I don't know what the heck I was even crying about! I feel a lot stronger having been through it and I think that's the key: you have to go through it to realize you can and you will survive. You have to witness your strength and resilience to know it's there at your disposal. Maybe the Girl Scouts need to make a new merit badge: "Bounced Back from a Breakup." If I had one, I'd wear it proudly.

10 THINGS THAT INSTANTLY CHEER ME UP
(NOT NECESSARILY IN THIS ORDER)

1. Music
2. Playing fetch with my dog
3. Singing and acting
4. My friends
5. My fans
6. Watching movies
7. Shabbat dinner every Friday with my family
8. Writing
9. A cup of coffee
10. Working out

Baby Steps

MAKE A FEEL-BETTER PLAYLIST

Music creates a pretty amazing soundtrack to life. It has the power to lift you anytime you're blue. I recommend creating a little pick-me-up playlist you can break out whenever you need it. Here's what's currently on mine . . .

1. "No Flag" by Nicki Minaj
2. "Copycat" by Billie Eilish
3. "Love Galore" by SZA
4. "Like That" by Bea Miller
5. "Love the Way You Lie" by Eminem, featuring Rihanna
6. "Roses" by Shawn Mendes
7. "Feeling Myself" by Nicki Minaj
8. "Life Is Worth Living" by Justin Bieber
9. "Drew Barrymore" by SZA
10. "A Little Too Much" by Shawn Mendes

#askAriel

I am the only one of all my friends who didn't pass their driver's test! I feel like such a loser!

Don't feel like a loser! I (still) can't drive and it's not the end of the world. Everybody is different, everybody learns differently, so if you have to take the test again or even a few times, there's nothing wrong with that. There's no stigma. If you didn't pass, it just means either you panicked (understandable) or you need more practice. I certainly know I do, and I wouldn't want to be responsible for my life and others' if I'm not feeling 110 percent confident in my skills. I will be totally honest with you: I am too scared to even *take* my driver's test because I know I'm *that* bad. So let's just say we will both put in some more practice behind the wheel and take the test when we feel ready to be on the road.

I can't believe it! I didn't make the cheerleading squad this year. I'm worried my cheer friends will disown me forever.

They will not disown you—not if they're really your friends. And if cheering is something that you're passionate about, don't give up. Work at it, then try again next season. Also, look at this as an opportunity: if you're not on the squad, you have more time to explore other hobbies and interests. You have a chance to branch out, broaden your horizons, even make some new friends. I know you're feeling disappointed because this took you by surprise, but see it as a blessing in disguise. Maybe this is the year you try out for girls' track? Or audition for the high school musical? This is your chance to be a whole new you. Look at me: I found a career when I gave musical.ly a whirl! I'm excited to see what's out there waiting for you and you should be, too.

I was going out with this guy for almost a year and I just found out he was cheating on me the whole time. What the hell? What do I do now?

You break up with him. Plain and simple. I know that sounds harsh, and it may hurt to do it, but this guy has disrespected you, lied to you, stabbed you in the back. He may beg and plead for you to forgive him and take him back; he may swear he will never do it again. I promise you, once a cheater, always a cheater. And from the sounds of your question, this wasn't a single, remote episode—it's been going on for a while. So let's review: he's broken your trust, he's hurt you, and he's shown that he has zero respect for your feelings or his commitment to your relationship. What makes him worth keeping around? Listen carefully: he does not deserve you, he does not deserve your love, and you deserve so much more.

PURPLE is the color of royalty and pampering. It reminds me that everything is better with a really nice manicure. . . .

Getting gorge

If you ask me how I define "beautiful," I honestly don't think it has much to do with what you've got goin' on on the outside. Instead, it's a quality that radiates from within— it comes from the content of your character. If you have a kind heart and you're a loving, good person, in my humble opinion, you're as beautiful as any Miss America or Victoria's Secret model. I see it—the question is, do you?

As teenagers, we generally have a tough time loving the image looking back at us in the mirror. Social media, as much as I hate to admit it, is partially to blame. We live in a time of posting selfies and videos for the whole world to see, and that makes us vulnerable to criticism. There's pressure to look good in those images, to have people comment "You're gorge!" and like your posts with hearts and flame emojis. But it's not only onlookers who are judgy; we are sometimes our own harshest (and most irrational) critic. I'm guilty of it: sometimes I stare at my lips and wish they were bigger. Would I like to be taller with thinner arms? Absolutely. But I wouldn't do anything drastic to change myself, and I know that a good lip liner, a pair of platform heels, and a cute jacket can do wonders. I try not to obsess over physical things and focus instead on the stuff that's more than just skin-deep.

When I was younger, around the time I was in middle school, if someone said they didn't like my hairstyle or my outfit, I became totally paranoid. I probably would have considered going home and changing rather than spend the day thinking I looked bad. Why? Because I was insecure. I didn't own who I was or feel particularly comfortable in my own skin, and, even worse, I was seeking approval from my peers. But I'll let you in on a little secret: the more confident you are, the less you care what others think or say, and the more you love yourself. It's taken me a while to arrive at this point, but now that I'm here, my life is much less complicated and I'm so much happier. I'm proud of all the choices I make, not just the popular ones.

Because I'm someone who always tries to be my authentic self. I choose to have real beauty role models, like Marilyn Monroe. I love her because, like me, she wasn't a size two or the skinniest of the skinnies. She had curves, she was thick, and I look up to her for that because that's how I am. I also love SZA because she's raw and real in everything she does, and she writes what she's feeling. Some people just have beauty in their soul. As a society, I definitely think that our image of beauty is changing for the better. People are becoming more accepting of others, more willing to embrace what makes us different. We come in so many shapes and sizes and colors, and we should always strive to appreciate them all. I love that someone curvy like Ashley Graham can be on the cover of the *Sports Illustrated* Swimsuit Issue, and James Charles can book a major CoverGirl campaign. We're also realizing that what we see on a magazine cover is likely photoshopped and filtered; there is no such thing as "perfect," not even if you're a supermodel or a movie star. We're human beings, not Barbie dolls! I guarantee that even the most beautiful person on the planet breaks out and gets bloated. If you are always retouching, filtering, skinnying your photos on Instagram, you're not embracing you true beauty, and you're certainly not letting others see it. I'm okay with waking up in the morning with bed head and no makeup on and posting a video or photo that's totally au natural. I want my followers to see the real me. Sometimes makeup feels like a mask, and I never want to hide who I am. By all means, glam yourself up if you feel like it—I love to play with makeup, I've never met a Sephora store I didn't like, and I've learned a lot of cool tricks from makeup artists and Patrick Starrr's YouTube tutorials. But just know that with or without the face paint, I love you (and you should love you) just the way you are.

Story Time

MY HISTORY OF HAIRTASTROPHES

I admit it: I change my hair *all* the time. It's another way I express myself and my creativity, so that's why at the moment it's jet black and I was blond a few months ago. When I decide to make the change, I try not to second-guess it. First of all, hair grows back, so you can cut it, dye it, curl it, straighten it, and, if you don't like it, it's completely fixable. My parents have always let me experiment for just that reason: it's not a lifelong commitment. If you highlight your hair and it looks weird, you can always go back to your true hue tomorrow (for the record, mine is dirty blond).

My hair and I have had a love-hate relationship. I think my most awkward phase was in second grade. I've always had big hair—not curly or wavy, more like fluffy and voluminous, but not in a good way. It just stuck out at all angles, like a big puffball sitting on top of my head. When it's long, the length weighs it down. But in second grade, I decided to cut it to shoulder length. Suddenly, my hair sprung up about six inches, and I literally looked like I had stuck my finger in an electrical outlet. My mom wouldn't let me use a straightening iron at the time because she was afraid I'd burn myself or my hair (I can't live without one now), so it just poofed out and was a total mess. I was eight years old; I don't think I realized at the time how bad it actually was. Little kids are kind of oblivious. But now I look back at old pictures, especially when we were going through albums and scrapbooks for this book, and I was like, "Oh my god, Mom! How did you ever let me out the door looking like that?" She insists it was cute. I'm horrified. I looked like a Q-tip.

In sixth grade, I Kool-Aided my hair. If you don't know what that is, allow me to elaborate: my friend and I decided to dip-dye our hair with red Tropical Punch Kool-Aid one day after school. Basically, you boil three packets of Kool-Aid in a large pot, give it a good stir, then pour the mixture into a bowl and dip your hair in it. I separated my hair into pigtails and basically held the ends in the hot liquid for about ten minutes, letting my blond hair soak up all that lovely fruit punchy color! After I blew it dry, I surveyed my look in the mirror. Yup, it was red. Cherry red. Kool-Aid red. Not very subtle, but definitely a different look for me. It took two weeks for the color to fade from fire-engine red to cotton-candy pink and eventually wash out altogether. I can't say I was too sad to see it go; it wasn't one of my finer hair moments. My brother and his friends are going through this stage now. Jacob's hair was purple last week and now it's green. Sometimes there are hits and sometimes there are misses, but it's a fun and harmless way to experiment, and I appreciate my parents letting us explore our hair color options!

A few years ago, I decided I wanted to go really blond— and thankfully this time I was smart enough to seek out professional assistance. I made a video about it, because sharing a potentially traumatic situation makes me feel so much better. As the camera rolled, I went to the mall, parked myself in the hair salon chair, and told the stylist to make me look a little more sun-kissed—nothing too crazy, just a shade or two lighter than my natural color. I sat back in the chair and was busy texting on my phone, checking my Instagram feed. When I looked up, my hair was covered in foils. I mean *dozens* of them. I started to really freak out.

"So, you remember how I said I wanted it to look natural, right?" I told the stylist.

"Uh-huh." She nodded, still painting away on my head. The highlight solution was a blue-white cream, and I could see her slapping on tons of it with a big flat brush.

"Well, that's a whole lotta highlights happening there," I pointed out.

"It's fine."

I gulped and hoped that my hair wouldn't look like I dunked it in a bucket of bleach. I prayed this lady knew what she was doing.

The worst thing about hair color is the wait—usually twenty to thirty minutes of letting the color develop, and during that time you have no idea what the outcome is going to look like. I stared in the mirror at my head full of foils—I had so much tin covering me, I looked like a roast about to go in the oven.

"Did ya check it?" I nagged the stylist. "Is it looking good? You're not leaving it on too long, right?"

Hair professionals don't really appreciate it when you try to tell them how to go about their business. But I was a basket case. I needed to know!

She peeled back a single foil and poked it with a fingered glove. "Not yet."

"Well, how much longer?" I continued prodding. "Like five minutes . . . or fifteen?"

"About twenty-five." Seriously? Only five minutes had passed on her timer? Was she sure it was working?

She handed me a magazine to read to take my mind off the wait. I flipped through the pages and saw Kylie Jenner on the red carpet in a platinum-blond wig. Oh my god! What if my hair looked like that? That wasn't exactly the look I was going for. . . .

The timer dinged and it was time to add toner, then wash it out. With my hair in the sink, I still had no clue about what it looked like. Then they wrapped it up in a towel. Were they purposely trying to make me crazy? When the stylist finally revealed my wet head, I could see a few blond highlights, mostly around my face and in the back, but not much of a change. "We'll dry it out and you'll see the difference," she assured me. "It'll be beautiful."

I watched as she worked her magic, blowing my hair out with a round brush so it fell in soft waves around my face. The color was exactly what I had envisioned: delicate sunny highlights that just brightened my face and made my hair look healthy and shiny. We even tinted my eyebrows lighter to match. I love, love, loved it and I completely forgot how stressed out I had been.

How I Do My Face
in Five Minutes

I'm all about simplicity, and I promise that you can do this makeup routine in record time, even if you're running late (like I usually am) in the morning. It's a nice, neutral, natural face. If you want more drama, add eye shadow, contour, or deepen your lip color. But this should be perfect for school or just hanging out; you'll look pretty, but not like you're trying too hard.

- **Prep your face.** I have mega-dry skin, so I start by applying a few dots of vitamin E oil to create a smooth canvas. You can also use your favorite moisturizer; my face is just dry as the Sahara and needs a bit more. But if you have acne-prone skin I would recommend a moisturizer with salicylic acid or for oily skin an oil-free moisturizer like Neutrogena's Sensitive Skin Ultra-Gentle Facial Moisturizer.

- **Next up: concealer.** I use it instead of foundation, dotting it under my eyes, around my mouth and nose, and on any zits that happen to pop up. The oil I applied first makes it easy to smooth. Right now, I'm loving Tarte Bare neutral concealer because it's very easy to blend. You don't even need a beauty blender or brush; your fingers are great tools.

- **Apply your lashes.** I love my fake lashes from MAC—they're long and wispy. It took me a while to master fake lash application without gluing my fingers together, but if you practice, it becomes easier and they won't look uneven.

- **Add a light coat of mascara.** Just to give your eyes a bit more pop!

- **Outline your lips with a lip pencil.** I usually use MAC Whirl because it's a shade that's close to my natural lip color. I overline just a bit to make them look larger. Fill in with a nice, sheer pinky lip color—I like Neutrogena Hydro Boost Lip Shine in Pink Sorbet or Soft Blush. Top with a shimmery lip gloss. I must own ten clear lip glosses and I'm always losing them, but one I haven't misplaced yet is Mary-Kate & Ashley Lip Crystals sheer lip gloss. I found it at my grandma's house one day and she was happy to let me keep it and it's become one of my favorites.

You can finish with a swipe of translucent powder in the T-zone to minimize shine and set it all in place, then you're good to go!

Baby Steps

10 TIPS FOR TAKING A GREAT SELFIE

There is a science to it; don't just point and click. Do a little prep first.

1. **Lighting is everything.** Make sure you have a good natural light source, and experts will tell you it should be in front of you, just slightly above eye level. If the lighting is too dark, your pic will look grainy and orange.

2. **Pay attention to the background.** Something interesting can really elevate your selfie. Nature or a cool painted wall is always a good choice for a backdrop.

3. **Play with your angles** and know your best side. If you turn your head slightly right or left, your features will pop more and won't look flat.

4. **Hold the camera slightly above your face,** so you're shooting down. This little trick makes your eyes look bigger and your jaw line stronger.

5. **Stretch your chin slightly out in front of you.** This will elongate your neck and make it more swan-like in your shot.

6. **Focus on one feature** you want to glam up and emphasize—not everything on your face. Go with either a sexy, smoky eye, a bold lip, or a shimmery highlight. All of the above equals overkill.

7. **Smile or at the very least smize.** Or show some kind of expression to add emotion behind the photo. Don't pout or do duck lips; that's so yesterday. A happy, cheerful expression is always prettiest.

8. **Don't overfilter or overedit** your picture so it

doesn't even look like you anymore. A natural shot lets the world see the real you (who is pretty fabulous!).

9. **Take selfies of stuff other than your face.** Like a cool pair of shoes or a pretty bracelet or a pretty manicure. Post anything and everything you're proud of.

10. **Invite someone to be in your selfie** with you. Grab a friend, your mom, your little brother—I always feel the more, the merrier!

#askAriel

I can't stop biting my nails, and I want long, gorgeous ones like yours. Any tips?

Um, yeah—get acrylics put on 'em, boo! At least until they grow a bit on their own, which they *will* underneath the fake ones (and in case you didn't know, my nails are fake!). The thing about fake nails, or acrylics, is that they're not all that great for your nails; they tend to make them weak. I think it's just a good way to get yourself into a no-biting groove, but not something you want to do all the time. I try to give mine a rest. Once you see how beautiful your nails look when they're not bitten to the quick, I think you'll want to quit your bad habit for good.

If you were stranded on a desert island, what is the one beauty product you couldn't live without?

If I'm stranded on a desert island, I promise you, I would

not be thinking about lip gloss or mascara. Hell no. I would be thinking about something that will save my butt till someone comes to rescue me—say, a big gallon of water or a flare to shoot off in the sky if a cruise ship is out in the distance. But if I have to choose cosmetics, then I guess I would say sunscreen. Those desert island rays can be pretty fierce, so I would want to make sure I'm covered. Probably SPF 100, and enough to cover my whole body, my face, my ears ('cause they burn pretty easily). And okay, maybe some ChapStick so my lips don't bake and flake.

I dyed my hair pink and my mom is freaking out and insists I dye it back immediately. But I really, really love it!

Okay, you may not want to hear this, but I'm going to tell it to you straight: you live in your mom's house, which means you have to follow her rules. I get that you don't agree with her in this case, but you may have to simply suck it up and respect her wishes—especially if you didn't get her permission in the first place and she hates surprises. If you love the look, there are a lot of ways you can still get it without going the whole dyeing route. You can use some pink clip-in extensions; you can get some Halloweenish spray-in color that washes right out; you can even get a wig à la Kylie and Gigi and just be pretty in pink for a party. If it's only a temporary situation, I think you'll get her to see it your way. But for now, just go back to your original color and keep the peace.

Conclusion

And you thought this was over?

Here we are at the end of my book, people . . . but that's just the thing. It's not the end; it's a new beginning. Every day is an opportunity to start fresh, be new, do you! I hope you're feeling pumped to go out there and put all your possibilities into motion. There are no limits unless you put them there. If someone asked me, "What do you want to be when you grow up?" I'd have to say, "Happy." That should always come first; it's the foundation that everything else is built upon. If you love what you do, things will magically fall into place: your relationships, your career, your path. By now, I hope you realize that happy is a choice you make, not something that you pick up at the mall. How you face obstacles and setbacks, how you see the world and your role in it, that's really all up to you. It kind of blows my mind to think that I will be able to vote in the next presidential election. The whole world will rest in our hands one day, and that's scary, but it's also really exciting and empowering. We could be the generation that makes all the difference. We could be the ones that bring about positive change in a big, big way.

I have learned a lot writing these pages. I've really pushed myself to dig deep and share my feelings with you, because I truly believe we're all in this together. Everything I have gone through in my life, I know I'm not the only one who's been through it. That said, no two people are exactly alike, so remember to embrace your individuality in as many cool, creative ways as you can. I can't imagine my life without all the colors of the rainbow in it. I can't picture who I would be if I wasn't *me*.

So let's play a little game: fast forward ten years. I'll be twenty-seven by then, which is not entirely a spring chicken, so I better be well on my way to where I want to be headed! If I close my eyes, I see myself married, hopefully with a kid or two, because I want to be a young mom who has lots of energy and likes to have fun adventures with her family. I want to be starring in a movie of my life—say, a romantic comedy/thriller—as well as writing and directing it, with Justin Bieber as my leading man. I want to be playing to sold-out stadium tours, winning Grammys for best album and pop song, and collaborating with SZA on a song and video. I want to be an activist, someone who doesn't just talk about what changes we need to make but actually fights to make them happen. I want to be living in LA in a big, beautiful house overlooking the Hollywood Hills, and I want my friends to come over for the most amazing pool parties every weekend. I want to be posting videos every day, probably on some new app that doesn't even exist yet—maybe I'll create one. I want to see the world, all of it. I want to be fearless and fierce and speak out, not just for myself, but for anyone who has ever felt overlooked and unheard.

Those are some pretty big dreams I just let loose. I want you to do the same. Just set them free into the universe; put them out there and see how far and fast they fly. . . .

✩ Acknowledgments ✩

This book has been a labor of love. I never could have imagined all the moving parts and details that go into completing a project of this magnitude, and I certainly couldn't have done it alone. I want to express my heartfelt gratitude to all the people who have guided and encouraged me throughout this process.

Alex Hoffman, I begin with you. I admire you for your kindheartedness and generous spirit. Your love, encouragement, and support inspired me to work hard and pursue my dreams. This amazing adventure couldn't have happened without you! And a big hug to Inga Bereza, Kudzi Chikumbu, Tiffany Matloob, and the rest of my musical.ly family, the world needs more people like you!

To all my #babies, you know who you are! I am forever grateful and indebted to you for sticking by me, keeping me sane and humble, and supporting each other! It fills my heart to see your videos and pictures, read your comments, and see how you have become a loving family. Thank you for accepting me as I am. I hope this book is a reminder to love yourself too and to follow your dreams.

Thank you Patrick Zielinski and Jessica Kelm and the Collab family, who believed in me from the very beginning. You guys took me under your wing when I didn't even have a clue about what I was getting myself into! Without your guidance I would never be where I am today.

A big thank-you to Sheryl Berk. You helped me get my journals, random thoughts, and incoherent babbling organized and onto the page. You made it natural and fun and it couldn't have happened without your guidance.

Thank you to Andrew Graham, Cait Hoyt, Jamie Stockton, Robert Mickelson, and everyone at CAA for believing in me; I'm proud to be a part of the CAA family and am so excited for the future.

To my legal team: Charlotte Towne, Adam Kaller, Ryan Pastorek, and Josh Binder. Thank you for always looking out for my best interests and reading between the lines for me.

Sara Sargent and the entire team at HarperCollins, this

is a dream come true and I am so appreciative of you taking a chance on me.

My incredible theatrical manager, Megan Silverman, your faith in me and your enthusiasm is contagious! I couldn't be happier to have you by my side and can't wait to see what more we can accomplish together.

The management team of Aton Ben-Horin and Ethan Curtis, I'm grateful for all you've done to steer me toward success.

To my closest friends, Arii, Daniel, Josh, Matthew, and Weston. You have been my rock through this crazy time. You've stood by me through the good times and through the bad. You've been a shoulder to cry on and the first people I've come to laugh with. Thanks for always being there.

To my dog, Bleu, thanks for the unconditional love, cuddles, and kisses and for listening without ever saying a word!

Thank you to my big, amazing, beautiful, crazy supportive familia: my aunts, uncles, cousins, and grandparents! No matter how insane life gets, nothing compares to coming home to the chaos and comfort of family.

To my partner in crime, my confidant, and constant companion, Jacob. I dedicate this book to you. You are my secret sharer and my best friend. I know I can always depend on you and you on me. I am so lucky to have you as my brother and I hope that we will always be close no matter how much distance is between us.

And finally, to my parents. Thank you. I could not have taken this journey without you both by my side. And more important, I wouldn't have wanted to. I am so grateful for your words of wisdom, your enduring faith in me, and the many sacrifices you have made so that I could chase my dreams. I hope you know how appreciative I am of everything you've taught me. Many of the stories and anecdotes written on these pages are inspired by you. I appreciate you allowing me to be me. Thank you for the endless nights of talks, advice, drying my tears, celebrating my successes, and catching me when I fell. Thank you for believing in me, reassuring me, and encouraging me to dream out loud!

I love you all.